P9-AGK-914

STRATEGIC PLANNING IN THE ARTS

Strategic Planning

in the Arts

A PRACTICAL GUIDE

Michael M. Kaiser

BRANDEIS UNIVERSITY PRESS Waltham, Massachusetts

Brandeis University Press

An imprint of University Press of New England

www.upne.com

© 2019 Brandeis University

All rights reserved

Manufactured in the United States of America

Designed by Richard Hendel

Typeset in Utopia by Passumpsic Publishing

For permission to reproduce any of the material in this
book, contact Permissions, University Press of New England,
One Court Street, Suite 250, Lebanon NH 03766; or visit
www.upne.com

Library of Congress Cataloging-in-Publication Data
available upon request

Hardcover ISBN: 978-1-5126-0174-9

Ebook ISBN: 978-1-5126-0321-7

5 4 3 2 1

This book is dedicated to John Spencer Roberts

CONTENTS

This book is intended to serve as a guide to those members of the staffs and boards of not-for-profit arts responsible for developing, evaluating, or implementing plans. When the first version of this book was written, almost twenty-five years ago, strategic planning was a relatively new concept for arts institutions. In fact, an argument had to be made for the importance of strategic planning. Today, most arts organizations embark on some kind of planning activity periodically. But a review of many hundreds of these plans suggests that most are simply a set of wishes rather than concrete plans for the future.

"We will increase ticket sales."

"We will do a better job raising money from corporations."

"We aim to attract a younger audience."

These are common "strategies" expressed in too many arts plans. Yet without any more detail about how ticket sales will be increased or more money raised, they are empty promises.

This book is intended to help arts institutions develop useful, implementable plans in efficient, well-organized planning processes. Planning today is more important than ever. Arts organizations face increasingly difficult resource acquisition and allocation problems resulting from new technologies, reduced arts education, aging donors, and new forms of entertainment. A coherent approach to these issues is essential if any arts organization is going to remain vibrant for a consistent period of time.

Developing these plans is not simple. As a result, many arts organizations that do attempt to develop strategic plans waste many hours because the planning processes they employ are not rigorous enough, are not well designed, or are poorly implemented. Just as success for an arts organization depends on a mix of creative vision and administrative expertise, so too does strategic planning depend on a mix of art and science. While creativity and insight are irreplaceable, the techniques of planning are designed to facilitate the development of insight. As in any discipline, when technique is ignored, creativity becomes difficult to channel.

Strategy development, however, is not a step-by-step process. While this book presents a sequential approach to planning, there is rarely one "correct" strategy that emerges from the planning process. The best planning processes allow for the iterations necessary for the best solutions "to hatch." In other words, while this book describes a practical approach to developing a strategy, it cannot teach how to think or to create.

STRATEGIC PLANNING IN THE ARTS

INTRODUCTION

I t is presumptuous, perhaps, to write a book about planning in the arts. The scarcity of talent and money has forced many arts executives to plan effectively and well in advance. The nature of arts planning, however, has traditionally been operational, focusing on such questions as, Who will be performing what role in which work directed by whom? What is often missing from planning in the arts is a strategic perspective: the development of an explicit mission for the organization, the analysis of the external and internal factors that affect the achievement of this mission, and the formulation of the direction that should, therefore, be pursued.

Strategic planning places operational decisions in a broader context. While operational planning determines who will sing the role of Aida, strategic analysis suggests the long-term implications of that casting decision for the organization. Will the hiring of a "name" singer sell more tickets? Will the audience come to expect famous singers? Will funders be impressed? Will your institution become more visible?

A direct result of this lack of strategic focus has been the rapid erosion in the financial bases of many arts organizations. Fiscal instability virtually always leads to reduced artistic programming. This, in turn, leads to deterioration in visibility, thereby limiting earned and contributed income. The resulting financial crisis consumes both the board and the staff, further restricting revenue and artistic flexibility. This vicious circle leaves artistic directors feeling frustrated, board members upset with the ever-increasing pressure to give and get more, and the administrative staff feeling powerless to handle mounting cash-flow problems.

While the serious lack of funding that triggers this chain reaction is frequently blamed on "the economy," it results more directly from a failure to recognize and react to changes in the environment. As the environment in which arts organizations have been operating has become far more challenging, the arts organizations that will survive, and even thrive, are doing more than complaining.

Virtually all major for-profit corporations, threatened with rapid technological change and mounting international competition, develop strategic plans. These corporations have realized that "working harder" is not enough to ensure future success. A review of the environment in which the business operates, coupled with an objective review of its own internal strengths and weaknesses, has proved to be essential to determining the most effective way to achieve corporate goals. In this respect, the needs of an arts organization are no different from those of a for-profit corporation. While the mission of an arts organization (or any not-for-profit organization) is more difficult to formulate, the benefits of developing a mission, analyzing the environment, and determining a strategy in response are identical. Organizations that do so find they have an easier time meeting their long-term objectives, fostering communication between their staffs and boards, and convincing patrons of their viability.

In specifying the plans and the planning process, it is essential to remember that even the largest arts organizations in the United States are small businesses. The Metropolitan Opera and the Metropolitan Museum of Art, the largest independent arts organizations in this country, would still not rank among the largest corporations in the United States. While small companies need planning as much as if not more than large corporations (they can't afford, after all, to waste anything), their approach to planning must accommodate their size: even small deviations from expected results can have major repercussions for small businesses.

As a result, arts organizations that find planning most useful are those that maintain an entrepreneurial perspective on planning and management, a willingness to make changes in course as experience and results dictate. Maintaining this entrepreneurial perspective is difficult, since there is an inherent tension between planners and entrepreneurs: planners expect fidelity to a predetermined course of action, while entrepreneurs demand the flexibility to change. A deeper understanding of the planning process reveals this tension to be superficial. Good planners expect and react promptly to changes in the environment. Conversely, the best entrepreneurs maintain a firm core vision. Specific operational steps might change; major strategic direction does not. While "entrepreneurial planning" is not easy, making the effort to develop a flexible, hence usable, plan is essential. The sad, but true, experience of many organizations, for-profit or not, that have tried planning is that bad planning costs more and returns less than no planning at all. A badly crafted plan leads either to the pursuit of the wrong path or, more frequently, to the discarding of the plan entirely. Either way, "planning backlash" —the feeling that planning is a waste of time—is the result.

Equally important for avoiding planning backlash is the development of a sensible planning process. When people are asked to spend hours and hours in unstructured, unproductive meetings, the perceived importance of planning begins to wane. Yet many successful, perceptive people endure these inefficient marathon sessions because they haven't experienced an efficient planning process and believe that planning is "good for them." When the resulting plan is ignored or discarded, frequently in short order, planning backlash emerges with full force.

In an effort to support planning in arts organizations, while avoiding planning backlash, this book addresses two major topics. The first part of the book reviews the content of a strategic plan. It proposes an approach to developing strategic plans with three distinct phases:

1. Setting up: Adopting the strategic framework that will guide the planning process and drafting a mission statement that motivates the entire plan
2. Analyzing: Collecting the data and performing the external and internal analyses that reveal the key strategic issues that must be addressed in the plan
3. Strategizing: Developing the artistic, administrative, and financial strategies that have the highest likelihood of achieving the organization's mission

The book concludes with a discussion of the process of developing a strategic plan, reviewing the steps that should be taken, the people who should be involved, and the formulation of a planning calendar. In short, the book begins by revealing what is in a plan and ends by suggesting the way the plan should be put together.

While many readers may feel inclined to turn to this second section first, one must caution that the key to a good planning process, like the key to good art, is a firm commitment to superior content. A rigorous planning process that does not produce a rich, comprehensive, *implementable* plan will certainly result in planning backlash.

PART 1 Setting Up

A FRAMEWORK FOR STRATEGY DEVELOPMENT
Building on the Mission

1

Strategizing is a creative process that cannot be performed simply by filling out forms. However, putting people in a room and asking them to think creatively about the future can yield very little and can waste a great deal of time. These sessions frequently devote too much time to the interests of a vocal minority, usually omitting discussions on many substantial issues and always prohibiting the development of a coherent, integrated plan.

Any planning process is made more efficient when it employs a structure, or framework, as a guide. This chapter introduces a framework that underlies one effective approach to planning. This approach is a generic one that has been used successfully by both for-profit corporations and not-for-profit organizations. Just as this framework provides a guide for the planning process, it will also provide an outline for this book. In the following chapters, each element of the framework will be tailored specifically to the needs of arts organizations.

THE MISSION STATEMENT

The foundation of this framework, and the starting point of all strategic planning, is the mission statement. The mission statement describes the central goals of the organization and the scope of its operations. The goal of a corporation in the for-profit sector is easy to describe: maximize stock price by making as much money as possible for as long as possible. While the mission statements for profit-oriented companies may include some discussion of the product line, customer base, or geographical scope, the central focus must be on profit. (Unfortunately, many for-profit organizations think of their missions as marketing statements, emphasizing specific products or services, or service to the customer, rather than profit. This can lead to a great deal of confusion when a corporation acts on behalf of its shareholders in a way that costs customers.)

For arts organizations, and all not-for-profit organizations, the mission statement is more difficult to define. We know the company is not in business to make a profit, but why does it exist? To offer world-class performances or exhibitions? To educate? To train young artists? To

7

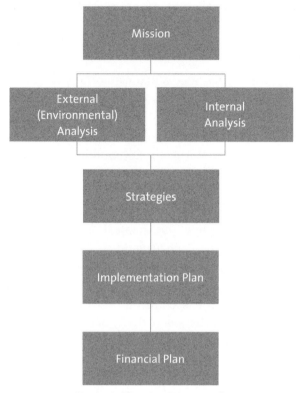

Strategic Planning Framework

serve a specific region? To encourage the creation of new works of art? To preserve and present older masterworks? When one removes the overwhelming profit motive, the mission becomes more difficult and, therefore, more important to formulate. For although the specific wording of the mission statement is not of key importance (too many people spend too much time worrying about the semantics of the statement), the implications of the organization's mission are staggering. They guide the entire planning process and, more important, should influence all programmatic and administrative decisions.

Those organizations without explicit missions have a difficult time managing themselves. Individual members of the staff or board may make decisions that they feel are best for the company but that counteract the actions of their peers; consistent progress in a missionless organization, therefore, is a result of luck.

If a mission statement is to be an effective management tool, every person who influences the behavior of the organization must understand its implications. For example, a symphony board that accepts world-class quality as an element of its mission must be willing to commit to raising the funds needed to achieve this huge ambition. Similarly, a regional theater company that aims to produce experimental works must be prepared to mount more targeted marketing and fund-raising efforts than a counterpart producing light comedies and musicals.

While the mission clearly directs the remainder of the planning process, the final wording of the mission statement need not be drafted before planning commences. The planning process is an enlightening, iterative procedure that allows the participants to "fine tune" the mission statement as they reveal the full implication of each parameter of that statement. However, while the final wording of the mission does not have to be determined in advance, a broad outline of the company's goals must be developed before any effective strategizing can commence. For without a goal, a strategy is meaningless.

ENVIRONMENTAL ANALYSIS

While a strategy without a goal is meaningless, a goal without a strategy is a wish. For this reason, developing a mission statement is not enough: expressing one's goals does not guarantee attaining them. Yet many organizations' plans are little more than a mission statement followed by several affirmations that the mission will be accomplished. ("The company will build its audience by improving its marketing program.") Clearly this is not sufficient.

The first step in determining how the organization will achieve its mission is to review the environment in which the company operates. No arts organization operates in a vacuum, despite the level of isolation its board and staff might feel. The success of an organization depends, in great measure, on the way it evaluates the environment in which it operates and its ability to respond appropriately. There are three parts to an environmental analysis.

The first is an evaluation of the arts ecology for the nation as a whole. What trends are going to affect the ability of an organization to achieve its mission? Are technological changes affecting arts participation? Is demographic change affecting whom we must address with our programming? A strong strategic plan must acknowledge explicitly the trends that are influencing the arts ecology.

The second aspect of environmental analysis is an exploration of the "industry" in which the company operates—the museum industry, the theater industry, and so forth. While many arts professionals may be uncomfortable with the word "industry," it is appropriate. Each art form offers products and services and has customers, competitors for resources, and suppliers—the participants that define an industry. This evaluation includes a review of peer organizations, those organizations that face similar opportunities and constraints and whose actions may affect one's own organization. For-profit companies study their competitors in order to predict how they will compete in the future. In the not-for-profit sector, competition is less direct. While the regional nature of the arts means that few arts organizations outside of major cities compete with other similar organizations for audience dollars or local contributions, they do compete with touring companies and for artists, gifts from national corporations and foundations, and grants from the National Endowment for the Arts, the National Endowment for the Humanities, and other government agencies. Increasingly, as arts organizations distribute their work online, competition between peer companies, even many thousands of miles apart, has intensified.

Of course, some cities do support multiple opera companies, symphonies, art museums, and so forth; in these culturally dense cities, direct competition is a more important factor. For this reason the third aspect of an environmental analysis is a study of the arts ecology of the city or region in which the organization operates. How many organizations are competing for earned and contributed dollars? How large is the base of corporate, foundation, and individual donors? What demographic, sociological, and economic factors influence the health of the arts institutions?

In sum, environmental analysis suggests the constraints and opportunities presented to the organization and indicates the factors required for success. In addition, this analysis will suggest how the environment is likely to change in the future. Understanding the evolution of the arts ecology in advance is a key to effective strategic planning because it gives the company time to decide on appropriate responses to expected environmental change.

INTERNAL ANALYSIS

Once an analysis of the environment has been developed, it is possible to evaluate the way one's own organization "fits" into the industry. This internal analysis is an integral part of the strategy development process. It suggests what the organization is doing well and what it is not doing well and how these strengths and weaknesses align with the success factors determined in the environmental analysis.

This internal audit is an essential element for creating a strong set of strategies. Yet internal analysis is difficult to perform because it demands objectivity in exploring areas of weakness and self-confidence in describing one's own strengths. By matching these internal characteristics with the industry success factors, one can identify those areas the organization must address in its strategic plan—both the strengths it can exploit and the weaknesses it must overcome.

STRATEGY DEVELOPMENT

An organization's strategies are a description of the way the organization expects to address the success factors revealed in the environmental analysis in light of the organizational strengths and weaknesses uncovered in the internal analysis. If the organization possesses one of the key success factors, how will it protect and exploit it? If the organization is deficient in another success factor, how will it overcome this weakness? The specific operating strategies that must be developed will depend on the nature of the organization, as illustrated by the following list of headings in the strategy sections for two organizations in differing industries:

DANCE COMPANY	MUSEUM
Artistic/repertory	Exhibitions
Production	Collection development/loans
Touring	Publications
Education programs	Education programs
School	Conservation
Development	Development
Marketing	Marketing
Finance	Finance
Administration	Administration

Personnel	Personnel
Volunteers	Volunteers
Facilities	Facilities
Technology	Technology
Governance/board	Governance/board

Virtually every organization, regardless of art form, will develop strategies for the same administrative functions; it is the programmatic functions that differ.

IMPLEMENTATION PLAN

Once the major strategies of the organization have been developed, one can produce an implementation plan. The implementation plan is a detailed work plan that assigns every strategy to someone and sets a time frame for its completion. This implementation plan gives board and senior staff a tool for ensuring that the plan is implemented. Without an implementation plan, most strategic plans end up sitting on a shelf, costing more than they deliver.

FINANCIAL PLAN

A final step in the planning framework is to translate the strategies into measurable financial results. While the ultimate goal of the organization is to achieve its mission, not to achieve a surplus, it is impossible to pursue a mission consistently if financial performance is not adequate. Therefore an attempt must be made to quantify the financial implications of each operating strategy. After a complete projection is developed, one can determine whether the financial results are acceptable. If not, a second iteration of the strategy development process should be initiated to suggest ways to improve financial performance.

This framework for strategy development, which leads from a mission statement to a long-term financial plan, is little more than structured common sense. Experience suggests, however, that organizations that use this framework, or similar ones, for strategy development develop effective plans in a most efficient manner.

2

A concrete mission statement is the foundation for the entire strategic planning process. It sets the standard to which the organization aspires, now and in the future, and forces board and staff members to align themselves around a specific agenda. When the mission statement is crafted in a rigorous manner, major disagreements can result, for this process requires making choices between size and quality, recognition at home and national prominence, education and performance, and art preservation and creation. This is not a bad thing. Out of this disagreement can come a clear and precise definition of goals that is the first step toward success.

There are no "correct" missions, and simply creating a statement that embraces the whole world of possibilities may be comfortable, or politically expedient, but it doesn't help create a clear path for the future. In fact, many arts organizations only truly address their missions when they experience financial distress and are forced to cut back. In good times, almost anything seems possible. The discussion concerning what to keep and what to discard when things get tough is really a mission development exercise.

While drafting a mission statement can often be a frustrating exercise in semantics, the effort devoted to developing the specific wording should not obscure the importance of delineating explicitly the goals of the organization.

One efficient way of writing a mission statement is to ask the board and senior staff members to make a list of all the potential elements of the mission. Parameters of the mission statement may include the following:

PRODUCT/SERVICE

What product or service does the organization offer? While this may seem obvious at first, many arts organizations offer a diverse set of services. Opera companies may produce live performances, online videos and podcasts, lectures, outreach programming, publications, recordings, and broadcasts. As the number of electronic transmission options increase, the definition of the company's "product line" will become a more complex issue. The mission statement must include a reference to those services that are essential to the organization.

REPERTORY

The organization must decide whether there is a specific repertory from which it will choose the works it produces. The Kronos Quartet, for example, presents a different repertory than the Juilliard String Quartet. It is important to note that while critics may give kudos for adventuresome programming, neither the Kronos Quartet nor the Juilliard String Quartet is "wrong" when it comes to repertory. Each company has specific strengths and faces unique constraints that influence its choice of repertory. Similarly, a museum must decide if there are specific areas in which it wishes to collect and exhibit. There are clear differences between the collecting missions of the Whitney Museum of American Art and the Pierpont Morgan Library.

QUALITY

What level of performance is desired? This is a very important and difficult decision to make. While every arts organization aspires to high quality, many organizations simply do not have the resources to perform at the highest level of quality. For example, it is unrealistic to expect a new contemporary art museum to build a world-class collection unless vast resources are available.

EDUCATION

How strong is the company's commitment to education? While this is a subset of the product/service decision, it deserves special mention. It is popular with many funders to stress a commitment to educate. However, one must honestly address the organization's commitment in this regard. Those companies with a true desire to educate must be willing to devote adequate resources and to identify the target recipients: The audience? Young artists? Children?

AUDIENCE

A substantial amount of effort must be devoted to determining the desired audience for each of the institution's services. Are the programs designed primarily for adults? For children? For a particular community? It is easy to say that the organization wants to serve everyone equally, but is that true? Is it doable with limited resources?

GEOGRAPHIC SCOPE

How much of the city/region/country/world does the organization hope to influence? The implications of this decision will have a tremendous impact on each element of the organization's operations. The mission statement should prioritize the importance of each relevant region. Remember that the organization need not serve every region in the same manner. The New York City Ballet offers regular live performances only in New York City, Washington, D.C., and Saratoga Springs yet serves the remainder of the country and the entire world with television broadcasts, online information, and occasional tours.

While the answers to these questions will guide the organization's entire planning process, the mission statement need not include references to all of the issues raised above. It should contain only the guiding principles of the organization. After creating the master list of possible mission elements, apply a simple test to each of them: ask whether the organization would be "satisfied" if it accomplished everything but that one element. If the answer is "yes," that element does not belong in the mission statement. If the company would not be fulfilled without accomplishing that one item, it belongs in the mission.

Typically, however, a strong mission will at least address what service the organization wants to provide, who is meant to be served, and some sense of the region to be served. While many arts leaders will be tempted to define these boundaries as broadly as possible, remember that the narrower the mission, the more the organization can focus its scarce resources. This is especially important for smaller arts organizations that do not have the staffing or financial resources to address a wide geography or set of services.

Despite differences in the substance of many mission statements, all superior mission statements should be

- Clear: There should be little room for interpretation; everyone reading the mission statement should come away with the same sense of its meaning. When a mission statement is filled with philosophical language, it makes it far more difficult to attain clarity.

- Concise: A short mission statement is easily remembered by staff, board, donors, and the public. A lengthy statement is hard to remember and, therefore, is likely not to guide the activities of the entire organization.
- Complete: The mission should address all the programming of the institution. Organizations that pursue programs not covered by their mission statements are guilty of mission drift. And when organizations violate their missions, they lose focus.
- Coherent: The mission must make sense and the various elements must be complementary. A theater company that performs avant-garde works but hopes to be the largest theater organization in a region is probably not going to accomplish both elements.
- Compelling: The mission statement should be phrased in a way that makes the goals of the organization attractive to others who may wish to be consumers, donors, volunteers, or board members of the organization.

For example, a regional theater company has developed the following mission:

> To establish a national reputation as a leading repertory ensemble theater company in our city that offers world-class theater productions and education programs especially to underserved audiences.

Notice that programs/services, educational programming, and quality level are mentioned, while fiscal performance and repertory are not. This simple statement makes it clear what the organization is trying to accomplish in general terms. Other organizations develop much more substantial statements of mission. It is frequently helpful to expand on the mission by listing a series of objectives. For this theater company, these objectives might include

- Increasing the number of productions offered;
- Developing new works;
- Producing a wide range of plays appealing to a variety of tastes;

- Exploiting all available performance formats including electronic media;
- Subsidizing ticket prices for certain audience members;
- Creating important theater education programs;
- Mounting vital outreach programs in underserved communities;
- Improving and expanding the apprentice and intern programs;
- Attracting the best directors and designers; and
- Providing theater to the entire community including productions that appeal to specific age, racial, and ethnic groups.

These goals provide a more concrete challenge to the board of directors and the staff of the organization and establish a clear starting point for the planning process.

A note of caution: try to avoid the following kinds of phrases in your mission statement:

- "Our mission is to ensure a balanced budget." This should not be the goal of a not-for-profit organization. The easiest way to achieve this goal is to shut down! It is undoubtedly true that we must not sustain deficits if we wish to accomplish our missions, but simply breaking even is not the true goal.
- "Founded in 1954 in Chicago . . ." The mission is not a history lesson; it is a set of goals for the future.
- "We offer three performances each year and do two outreach programs in our community." It is dangerous to discuss *how* the organization achieves it goals; these can, and probably should, change with some frequency as the environment changes around us.

PART 2 Analyzing

UNDERSTANDING THE ENVIRONMENT
External Analysis

3

Since the early 1970s, it has become very fashionable to use the modifier "strategic" whenever one discusses planning. While it may seem sophisticated to talk about "strategic" planning or "strategic" marketing, few people using the word know its meaning. What turns old-fashioned, "long-range" planning into "strategic" planning is the explicit analysis of the environment in which the organization operates. Just as a football coach cannot develop a game plan without clear knowledge of the field and the competition, so too an arts organization cannot develop a plan without understanding what is happening around it.

For an arts organization, a thorough review of the environment includes three distinct activities: analyzing the arts environment nationally, understanding the constraints and requirements for success of the individual art form, and evaluating the specific city or region in which the organization operates.

NATIONAL ARTS TRENDS

It is impossible to assess the environment in which an arts institution operates without analysis of the trends that are affecting all arts institutions in the nation and, perhaps, the world. In fact, the arts ecology has changed dramatically over the past twenty-five years.

After a period of growth in the number and potency of arts institutions in the second half of the twentieth century, several trends are conspiring to make it more difficult for arts organizations to prosper. These include the following:

- A radical reduction in the amount of arts education in the public schools. This has made it far more difficult to attract new audiences, since so many young people have not had a comprehensive arts education. In the long term, arts organizations will also have a harder time finding people willing to serve as donors, board members, and volunteers, since fewer adults will have had the background in the arts that motivates them to participate.
- Gradual reduction in the number of people willing to subscribe to

an arts organization. As ticket prices have risen, work travel has increased, and more women have built careers outside the home, it has become increasingly difficult to get audience members, even loyal ones, to be willing to buy tickets to a group of performances, in advance. While subscriptions were once responsible for the majority of ticket sales, most arts institutions are satisfied if one-third of their tickets are now sold by subscription. This has increased the cost of marketing (since selling each performance individually costs more than selling a package), eliminated much of the financing provided by advanced subscription ticket purchases, and made it more difficult to include adventuresome work in a season (since each work must now be sold on its own merits).

- The aging of our traditional major donor base. In most cities, a handful of individuals have been the flagship funders for arts organizations. As these donors age, they are turning over their families' philanthropic decisions to a new generation of individuals who may not be as passionate about the arts as their parents have been. This is leading to major reductions in contributions from these families.

- New forms of entertainment and education. Over the past twenty years, entirely new forms of entertainment and education have become available at very low cost. From computer games to YouTube, Facebook to MOOCs, and Netflix to Twitter, people now enjoy a range of online activities that reduce the time available for attendance at museums or performances. These activities have also trained people to expect entertainment on demand, at whatever location is convenient. Many arts organizations are exploiting these technologies to distribute their work to a larger audience; this places smaller, less visible institutions at a distinct disadvantage and calls into question the sustainability of many midsized arts organizations whose work is not as distinguished as needed to compete with online offerings from internationally renowned organizations.

- Reduced professional critical coverage. While there are now innumerable ways for individuals to provide criticism of exhibitions and performances, far fewer newspapers and television stations are employing professional critics who bring great knowledge and experience to their reviews.

These trends are real and are affecting the options available to arts organizations today. A strong strategic plan must explicitly address these trends and others that the planner may identify. How will these trends affect your organization? What other trends have you identified? How can your organization take advantage of new opportunities and overcome challenges to create a strong, vibrant institution?

ART-FORM-SPECIFIC TRENDS

While these trends affect every arts institution, there are other trends that affect arts institutions only in specific art forms or groups of similar organizations. For example,

- Art museums are facing a dramatic surge in interest in contemporary art, especially from the newly wealthy who are building their own collections. This has placed pressure on encyclopedic museums to bolster their contemporary holdings.
- Arts organizations of color are more reliant on foundation funding than their Eurocentric peers that get more funding from individual donors. As organizations of color maximize their foundation revenue, they must begin to build stronger individual giving efforts and attract stronger boards if they are going to continue to thrive.
- Opera companies are facing changes in taste and lifestyle that makes it less attractive to spend four hours watching a performance. Pop-up opera and new operas are on the upswing.
- Symphony orchestras must address the dramatic reduction in the potency of recording companies that had traditionally done substantial marketing of solo artists and conductors. Now symphonies must increase the amount of marketing they do for their guest artists to build demand.

A strong environmental analysis will reveal the trends that are facing your industry and discuss implications for future strategies.

Evaluating an arts sector continues with a review of the structure of the industry, that is, a systematic look at the key industry participants. The simplest way to reveal the structure of an industry is to use a model developed by Michael Porter of the Harvard Business School. This model has proved to be as relevant to arts industries as it is to the for-profit

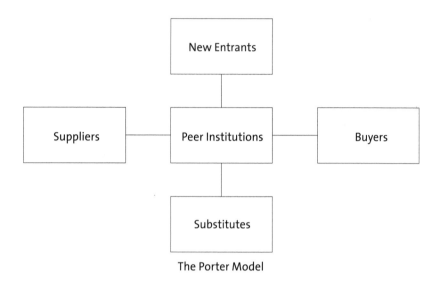

The Porter Model

sector. It separates industry participants into five key categories, including the following:

Peer companies — Those organizations that offer the same level of product or service and therefore compete for resources, customers, and patrons. The Chicago Lyric Opera and the San Francisco Opera are peer companies. Small, local opera companies do not use the same level of singer, designer, orchestra, and so forth, and are not peer companies of either of these two larger organizations.

New entrants — New organizations that might become peer companies in the future. For example, several serious theater companies have started operations in Philadelphia over the past twenty years. Their opening has had a major impact on the city's senior theater organizations, since the companies compete for many of the same donors, audience members, plays, and artists.

Substitute products	Those products or services that offer an alternative to the customer. There are several levels of direct and indirect substitutes. HD opera shown in movie theaters is a direct substitute for live opera. Movies are an indirect substitute for opera performances.
Buyers	Most arts organizations must market to, and compete for, three kinds of "customers." Clearly, those people who buy tickets for performances, exhibitions, and so on, are one important set of buyers. A second set of buyers is the presenters that engage performing arts organizations for tours, or museums that rent shows from other museums. A third group of buyers is contributors who support the activities of the organization. While their "purchases" are less concrete, contributors, like ticket buyers, give money to arts organizations and receive something in return.
Suppliers	The artists, technicians, and other personnel who provide their services to an industry, as well as other suppliers of materials, venues, and so forth.

Each of these five groups of participants creates tension in an industry; the magnitude of these tensions will determine the difficulty of sustaining financial health and artistic performance in that industry. If there is a great deal of competition among peer companies, if the potential for new entrants is strong, if buyers and suppliers are powerful, and if substitutes are numerous, then industry participants are going to have a difficult time sustaining a high level of performance.

Most not-for-profit theater companies suffer from this difficult industry environment. Since creating a new theater company is relatively easy, there are many new companies formed each decade. The large number of choices between theater company offerings and numerous substitute products (movies, television, Netflix, other performing arts, etc.) makes the ticket buyers extremely powerful and makes it difficult to attract substantial funds from contributors. While the oversupply of acting talent makes suppliers "weak," name performers have a great deal of clout and can create high costs for theater companies that employ them. This combination of easy entry, strong competition, buyers and suppliers, and numerous substitutes creates a terribly difficult environment in which to operate. Note that this analysis refers only to an industry as a whole; there may be one or more organizations that have built strong positions that allow them to thrive even in a difficult environment.

In most industries, the problems are not this severe but one or more of these factors do present a problem; isolating the factors that create the problem is crucial to identifying the solution. For this reason, it is productive to review each set of participants in some depth.

PEER INSTITUTIONS

If more than one organization offers a similar product to the same buyer group, the industry becomes substantially more "difficult." For this reason, it is important to understand those peer organizations that might influence your industry segment.

While the analysis of peer organizations can yield a significant amount of information for strategic analysis, peers affect an industry structure only to the extent that they provide direct competition for patrons, customers, or suppliers. (In fact, in the for-profit sector, peer company analysis is termed "competitive analysis," a direct name that is considered inappropriate for the more harmonious arts community.) Most arts companies secure regional funding and sell to local audiences and, therefore, are not affected by most peer companies.

Even "national" organizations (e.g., New York Philharmonic and Chicago Symphony Orchestra) do not compete directly for ticket sales. They do compete for some funding, although most arts patrons tend to be regionally focused as well. (This trend is changing and is providing for increasing competition in many arts industries.) Thus, there is very little direct competition for income between the Chicago Symphony and the New York Philharmonic. There is substantial competition between these two organizations—and numerous other orchestras throughout the world—for the services of soloists and conductors, however, and increasingly, they compete for attention online. In most cities, with only one major participant in each art form, direct competition comes more from touring companies and from substitutes.

In cities with more than one major opera company, museum, and so forth, the impact of peer organizations is greater than in cities with less "cultural density"; ticket sales will be harder won and fund-raising will be more competitive. This does not mean that analysis of peer companies is not useful for regional arts organizations. Instead, peer company analysis becomes more informational and less strategic, providing insight into the way a similar organization operates rather than how that organization's activities will affect one's own performance.

NEW ENTRANTS

If the number of peer organizations increases, the competition for artists, audiences, and donors will similarly increase. For this reason, the number of new participants in an industry has a considerable impact.

In most arts disciplines, it is unlikely for a large number of new entrants to emerge owing to the high cost of establishing a presence. Opera companies, ballet companies, symphonies, and museums tend to face few new entrants and, hence, less direct competition. In those art forms where costs are lower—modern dance and chamber music—one is more likely to see a significant number of new companies. It is very easy to establish a poetry reading organization; one needs only a public space. This has led to a high level of competition for a very small group of buyers, a very difficult environment for established literary organizations.

Those factors that make it expensive or difficult for a new organization to perform successfully are termed "barriers to entry." For example, the time and cost required to establish a unified ensemble quality in ballet and symphonic music serve as substantial barriers to entry. Similarly, the cost of mounting grand opera prevents the establishment of new companies. (Not surprisingly, many new concert opera groups, that offer "un-staged"—therefore, less costly—versions of operas, have been established in recent years.) And the high cost of building both an important collection and a suitable facility makes it extremely expensive to establish a major new museum.

This does not imply that museums, opera companies, ballet companies, and so forth, are "protected" from all new entrants. New "competitors" may be formed, but substantial resources will be necessary. The

Broad Museum in Los Angeles, for example, has had a major impact on all museums of the region. Frequently, national companies on tour pose the biggest threat of entry to regional performing arts organizations. While these may not represent new organizations, they may be new to the region. Although touring companies do not often compete directly for contributions, they do compete for ticket sales. And in most cases, a local presenting organization does compete for funding with those local organizations that self-produce. The Metropolitan Opera used to present an annual spring tour following its New York season. This tour represented the biggest competitive threat to many regional opera companies. Since the tour has been canceled, these local companies have had an opportunity to solicit the local ticket buyers and funders of the tour.

SUBSTITUTES

Ballet companies do not compete only with other ballet companies, nor do opera companies compete only with opera companies. Art forms compete with each other and with other forms of entertainment and leisure time activities for ticket buyers and for patrons. The presence of substitute products affects arts organizations as much as the sale of tea affects coffee merchants.

Companies face both direct and indirect substitutes. Ballet, symphonic music, opera, and the like, are direct substitutes for each other. There are many similarities among these types of performances and among the people who attend them. Indirect substitutes include other forms of entertainment: television, radio, sports, and so forth. It is essential to identify those substitutes that provide the greatest challenge before one can create a strategy to overcome them.

A new form of substitute, and an increasingly important one, is electronically distributed performance and education programs. Symphonies have had to compete with recordings for decades; now other performing arts companies are facing competition from online arts and other forms of entertainment. The difference between watching live performances and online performances is substantial. However, the cost of online performances is so low, and the cost of live performances and the ancillary expenses of attending a live performance—babysitters, parking, and so on—are rising so rapidly that many people may decide to "attend" the opera in their homes. (This could be a particular problem in those cities where the local arts companies do not employ the "name" performers typically featured in electronic performances.)

While online arts will not eliminate the demand for live performances, the need to improve quality and the pressure to keep a rein on price inflation will build for all arts organizations as world-class broadcasts produce a widespread standard for performances. Museums are not immune; many institutions have made their entire collections available online, and others are offering movie theater "tours" of their major exhibitions.

BUYERS

As mentioned above, arts organizations typically serve three major sets of buyers: purchasers of tickets or classes, presenters of touring groups or exhibitions, and contributors. Ticket purchasers and students traditionally form the largest group of buyers. As one evaluates the strength of these buyers, one must determine the choices available to them, their dedication to the art form, and their sensitivity to price increases. Each of these factors will have a major impact on the industry.

A simple audience survey can be most helpful in addressing these questions. In addition to revealing the demographics of the ticket buyers and the best ways to market to them, surveys help to determine the value buyers place on the repertory chosen, the importance of recognizable performers, the importance of high production values, and the need for amenities (parking, restaurants, etc.).

The results of an audience survey must be used carefully. In many arts organizations, great tension arises from the dichotomy between artistic priorities and the audiences' tastes. Marketers/administrators will often encourage programming of well-known, accessible works (with a famous guest star) while the artistic staff wants to try something new and experimental. (This is a particular problem in smaller cities where the audience for experimental works may be small and dispersed.)

No arts organization should change its mission solely because of its audience's interests. An organization aiming to produce experimental theater but selling to ticket buyers who want musicals is either marketing to the wrong audience or needs to pursue a major educational effort, or both. However, it is equally important for the artistic and administrative leadership of an organization to understand the interests of its audience and to be realistic about the potential for growth and even survival if the mission and audience tastes are hopelessly divergent. The most congenial situation, of course, is when the mission of the organization is consonant with the desires of its audience.

Audience surveys will also indicate the level of price sensitivity of the ticket buyers, giving a first approximation of the amount of business an organization may lose if it raises ticket prices.

Typically, since very few arts organizations market to homogeneous groups, there will not be one simple answer to any survey question; buyers will tend to be grouped by type. It is important to understand the needs and desires of each buyer grouping, or niche. Sometimes, individual marketing strategies can be developed that address the needs of a particular market niche without adversely affecting other buyers. For example, many performing arts groups have experimented with "singles' nights" that offer unmarried adults the chance to attend performances and postperformance parties with their peers. This has built larger audiences without affecting the programming prerogatives of the artistic staff.

Institutions—for instance, presenters who "purchase" a company for one or more performances or one museum contracting to mount an exhibition produced by another museum—are a second buyer type. Since their purchases are so large, these buyers are more powerful than individual ticket buyers and consequently have a greater ability to influence repertory and to demand reduced fees. The extent to which any buyer, individual or institutional, has power will depend substantially on the popularity of the organization. When the Bolshoi Ballet tours, it can demand and receive complete artistic control and substantial fees and still repeatedly perform to sold-out houses. A small regional ballet company typically does not have this freedom.

A third set of "buyers" is the contributors to the organization. Just as it is important to determine what ticket buyers value, it is also vital to understand why donors support the institutions in the industry and the level of their commitment. Each of the key contributor groups should be reviewed, including government, foundation, corporate, and individual donors. Trends in contributions and key donor priorities should be evaluated.

In the museum industry, for example, support from individual and corporate donors has grown far more rapidly than support from government agencies over the past decade. Not surprisingly, museums have become more responsive to the wishes of these donor groups. The importance corporate donors place on visibility has been a major reason for the increasing importance of "blockbuster" exhibitions: large-scale exhibitions that guarantee substantial attendance because of the popularity of the subject matter.

SUPPLIERS

While buyers are responsible for industry income, suppliers are responsible for industry costs. Many companies are faced with direct competition from peer companies (and indirect competition from film companies, recording companies, etc.) for their performers. This is especially problematic in the opera industry where the number of singers with a major reputation is quite small and fees, therefore, can be staggering.

The problems of the opera industry were traditionally exacerbated by the alternative sources of employment for opera singers, especially recordings. In recent years, the decline of the recording industry has reduced the "power" of star singers; this alternative form of employment is now harder to come by, and the missing marketing clout of the recording industry means fewer opera singers develop huge reputations. Not surprisingly, ballet dancers have tended to earn substantially less than opera singer, since alternative forms of employment are less readily available. Ballet dancers' bargaining power is further reduced, since they tend to commit themselves to one company, and one dance technique, for an extended period of time. As a result, even principal dancers with major companies do not get to renegotiate their fees with the same freedom as opera singers who may perform with many companies in one season.

Of course there are many other suppliers to each art form, including stage labor, set designers, costumers, curators, administrators, teachers, and venues. Each of the major suppliers to an industry must be reviewed to determine whether it presents a problem to the organizations in the industry and whether a strategy must be developed to overcome this problem.

CITY-SPECIFIC RESEARCH

While understanding industry trends in a sector of the arts ecology is vital, so too is understanding the locality in which the organization operates. Despite the growth of online arts, the arts are still predominantly local.

Key issues to be addressed include the following:

- Demographics: What is the nature of the population of the city/ region, and how is this changing? Arts organizations must evaluate the demand for their work in relation to the population they are hoping to serve.
- Cultural density: How many arts institutions are competing for audiences and funding? In culturally dense cities, arts institutions must be able to build distinct profiles and assemble strong boards to compete for funding and audiences.
- Concentration of funding: Do a few donors dominate the giving landscape? In cities with high donor concentration, arts institutions must either find a way into the hearts of these funders or be willing to do the missionary work required to build new donor groups.
- Traffic patterns: Do traffic or parking concerns play a role in determining arts attendance? Arts institutions in cities with major traffic problems must compete more against online activities that allow people to enjoy the arts at home.
- Corporate headquarters: Are there a number of corporate headquarters in the city/region? It is increasingly difficult to obtain corporate donations, especially in cities with few corporate headquarters.
- Tourism: Is there a large base of cultural tourists? While tourists can be more expensive to reach, arts organizations in cities with large tourism sectors have a new group of potential ticket buyers every week.

SUCCESS FACTORS

In addition to suggesting the challenges and opportunities that will face an arts organization, environmental analysis reveals those characteristics that will be required for an organization in that industry to succeed.

Isolating these success factors is crucial to the entire planning process. If we know what an opera company must have to be successful, we can focus our planning on developing that asset.

For example, an analysis of corporate donors suggests that visibility is becoming increasingly important to them. As ownership of corporations is increasingly spread over a large geography, most corporations no longer choose to give away money simply to be good citizens; increasingly, the marketing departments of corporations are becoming involved in giving decisions. For this reason, many arts organizations are challenged to enhance public awareness of their programs and services.

If new entrants are establishing themselves, this will increase "competition" among peer companies for ticket sales and contributions. This increased competition will require more expenditures on making the company seem different from others—a sophisticated marketing program supporting a strong artistic vision will be increasingly important in the future.

If a substitute technology is becoming more of a factor, one must decide whether the industry should embrace the new technology. The Metropolitan Opera has had great success adapting to technological advances: first with its radio broadcast, followed by television, video cassettes, DVDs, Met Titles, and HD movie theater broadcasts. This "beat 'em or join 'em" decision requires a great deal of careful planning.

If suppliers are a problem, one must decide whether to accept the restrictions or find substitutes. Obviously, if the key suppliers are the artists, only a change in artistic vision will accommodate a change of suppliers, and the vision should never change solely on the basis of a planning analysis! However, if the problem is the supplier of other materials or services, frequently a change in suppliers will not affect the product.

Industry analysis does not reveal the optimal strategy, but it efficiently isolates the area that needs to be addressed. Armed with a clear understanding of their environment, planners have a substantial head start in constructing the optimal strategic path for their own organizations.

INTERNAL ANALYSIS
The Management Audit

4

While the external analysis suggests the constraints and opportunities presented by the environment, the internal analysis reveals the strengths and weaknesses of a particular organization. Matching the results of the internal analysis with the requirements for success revealed in the industry analysis identifies those areas of strategic concern. If one key for success for a modern dance company, for example, is a strong touring program, a nontouring organization must address this shortcoming explicitly in its strategic plan. Conversely, a company with a thriving tour program should strategize to protect this important asset. This does not imply that every modern dance company should have the same strategy or should aim to operate in one prescribed manner. Rather, a modern dance company that cannot, or chooses not to, tour must accept the consequences of that decision.

As with peer company analysis, each element of the company's operations should be scrutinized. While it is obviously easier to obtain more data for internal analysis than for peer company analysis, it is far more difficult to interpret those data objectively. Some organizations rationalize away any negative reviews, fund-raising shortfalls, or earned-income problems. Others are too critical of their own capabilities, believing that other organizations do everything better. A strong plan depends on an honest appraisal of weaknesses and strengths; nothing is gained from being overly generous with praise, nor is there any point to self-flagellation.

There are several effective approaches for performing an internal analysis. The first is to evaluate how the organization has developed compared to industry norms. While no two arts institutions mature in exactly the same manner, many develop in a similar series of stages.

STAGE ONE: THE DREAM

Virtually every arts organization begins as the dream of a visionary. The goal may be lofty ("providing access to great art to people of all backgrounds") or more personal ("providing an opportunity to show my work") or some combination of the two.

Artists who decide to leap into self-production will follow very different paths, depending upon two vital characteristics: talent and money. Great artists, at least those who are perceived by the world as great artists, can build an earned-income base and, eventually, a contributed income base as well. Those artists with sufficient financial backing can "buy" some measure of success. These lucky few (and they are getting fewer and fewer each year) can establish a board of directors, receive bookings, sell tickets, and raise funds. If they approach these activities in an organized manner, they can mature in a rather painless fashion.

But most artists who launch organizations do not have this bounty and must start with little acclaim and less money. They will typically save up for one initial project, frequently with the support of family and friends. The project goes well, everyone offers positive feedback (except, perhaps, the critics, who may pay no attention whatsoever), and the artist is convinced that the applause will go on forever.

STAGE TWO: THE REALITY

Then reality sets in. All funds were used for the first project. No one is knocking down doors to offer bookings or money. And the thought of doing it all again is daunting.

Many artists stop at this point and return to employment with an established arts organization. Others persevere and enter a critical stage in the development of their companies: they come to appreciate the nonartistic elements of arts production. Marketing, fund-raising, tour booking, finance, boards of directors, and even planning become real and important.

How the artist copes with this set of issues will determine, in many respects, the way the company will develop. Creating a strong board that can provide and solicit funding and can help address administrative requirements is crucial. Building an arts organization is expensive; without access to substantial resources of their own, artists must rely on others. Typically, artists will limp along from season to season, without significant growth in support, ticket sales, or artistic scope. In fact, most start-up arts ventures become mired at this stage and then eventually evaporate from lack of funding or persistence.

The fortunate few who can attract a strong board, hire a talented administrator, make an impression on critics and audiences, begin to receive support from foundations or corporations (usually through board contacts), and make it through this arid period with determination intact will enter the most exciting phase of their organizational careers.

STAGE THREE: GROWTH

After several years of presentations, a well-managed, successful arts project will enjoy a level of demand, a degree of visibility, and a base of support that provide the seeds of a lasting organization. Typically, at this time, audiences build, the family increases in size—gifts from individuals grow substantially and foundation support and government grants commence—visibility expands, and touring opportunities increase. This confluence of visibility, institutional support, and earned-income growth allows the organization to flourish. The hard work of the board begins to pay off, money flows more freely, the administrative infrastructure can be strengthened, and management looks like a group of heroes.

STAGE FOUR: STAGNATION/CRISIS

The euphoria of the growth period comes to a crashing halt when the company has maximized its income from core funders, the board members are no longer increasing their gifts to match the organization's budget growth, and earned income hits its peak (especially if the artistic programming loses its edge).

Suddenly, the rapid annual increases in expenses enjoyed during the growth phase are no longer matched by increments in revenue. Since this turn is rarely anticipated, arts organizations typically incur one to three years of deficits during this stage. If the deficits are large enough, they can erase all accumulated surpluses and even threaten the life of the organization. The lack of a financial cushion is perhaps now most evident; the organization is as famous as it ever was, but it is in danger of extinction. Management invariably is blamed, the board grows frustrated, the artistic mission is ignored, and cash flow becomes the central topic of conversation.

These problems call for substantial institutional change: improving development capability, building institutional visibility, strengthening the board, and so forth. Organizations that recognize this are in a good position to move past the crisis point. Those that fail to see the need for change, or believe they can grow stronger by continuing to reduce budgets, tend to wither away.

STAGE FIVE: THE INSTITUTION

Organizations that emerge from the crisis (and the rare few able to avoid it altogether) can become true institutions with the board and staff needed to foster consistent artistic accomplishment and the earned and contributed income base needed to support program development.

These institutions are not immune to problems and must stay aware of environmental changes. But with the proper mix of artistic and administrative leadership, and the oversight of a strong, continuously evolving board, these organizations have the potential to weather crises by building financial structures, including endowments, which provide long-term stability.

The Alvin Ailey American Dance Theater is just one of many arts organizations that proceeded through these stages. It was founded in 1958 by Alvin Ailey and Carmen de Lavallade when they were dancing in a Broadway show. They rehearsed their dancers before and after performances on the Broadway stage. Creating an arts institution that would last fifty years was truly a dream. Initial performances at the Ninety-Second Street YMHA (Young Men's Hebrew Association) in New York City were well received. But creating a permanent corps of dancers was challenging. Through the 1960s and 1970s, the company grew; Ailey created works including *Revelations* and *Cry* that inspired audiences and funders. But the growth of the organization's reputation was not always matched by growth in financial strength. By the late 1980s, the organization was struggling with major cash deficits and with Ailey's untimely passing in 1989. Judith Jamison, the new artistic director, led a turnaround effort that stabilized finances, restructured the board, established a far larger family of donors, and allowed the organization to build a new home in New York City and become the institution it is today.

While each arts organization develops in its own unique way, this normative model provides a context for internal analysis. Indeed, by isolating ways in which an arts organization strays from this typical path, one can learn a great deal about its idiosyncrasies—both its peculiar strengths and weaknesses. For example, an organization that has grown substantially but has failed to build its board is likely to have a fund-

Table 1. Organizational Stages of Development: Comparison Chart

	Stage One: The dream	Stage Two: The reality	Stage Three: Growth	Stage Four: Stagnation/crisis	Stage Five: The institution
Programming	Self-produced Single-project focus Artist driven	Self-produced Single-project focus Artist driven Company size remains small	Increased touring High production values Increased program resources Earned income increases	Earned income levels off "Fundable" projects developed Programs retrenched	Vital/well rounded programming High production quality
Funding	Personal funds Friends/family Minimal fees from presenters	Limited foundation funding Small gifts from individuals Corporate matching gifts	Large individual gifts Initial government funding New/larger foundation support Corporate gifts Membership drive	Institutional sources maximized Board unable to increase personal gifts	Stronger support from individuals Planned giving programs Multiyear institutional gifts Access to corporate underwriting
Marketing	Word of mouth Cards/posters Modest ads if any	Word of mouth Cards/posters Modest ads if any	Advertising program initiated Group sales Subscription program	Marketing program cut to reduce budget	Institutional visibility required Better packaged "product"
Finance	Cash driven	Bookkeeping required Need to "manage" cash Annual budgets	Careful budget preparation and monitoring Financial reporting improved	Expenses greater than revenues Substantial payables accrued Board/bank loans to meet cash flow needs Financial analysis refined	Stabilization tools required • Cash reserves • Endowments • Real estate

Table 1 *(continued)*

	Stage One: The dream	Stage Two: The reality	Stage Three: Growth	Stage Four: Stagnation/crisis	Stage Five: The institution
Board	Small Friends of artistic director Serve legal needs Volunteer staff Some financial support	Small Friends of artistic director Serve legal needs Volunteer staff Some financial support	More financial support Effort to identify funding prospects Committees formed	Financially "tapped out" Inadequate access to gifts Demand cutting costs Board feels ineffective	Maturing/ improving Organized committees Accepts fundraising responsibility Monitors financial performance closely "Experienced" board members
Staff	No administrative staff Artists/board do everything	No administrative staff Artists/board do everything Some staff may be required	Staff departments formed Greater staff- board activity	Staff/board tensions Survival an issue again Morale problems	Formal management structures

raising profile that is weak on individual giving. An organization that has been able to develop a cadre of very loyal donors, but has not created the size family normally associated with an organization of its size, is vulnerable as the donor base ages. Clearly the plans for these two organizations must address these shortcomings. These revelations should form the heart of the internal analysis.

COMPARISON CHARTS

Another method for isolating areas of interest for your organization is to produce an analysis that reveals how one's own organization and one's peers differ from industry norms for selected important parameters. Each industry association (e.g., Dance USA and Association of Art Museum Directors) publishes substantial data for the industry and for individual organizations. DataArts (formerly the Cultural Data Project) also collects financial information from numerous arts institutions.

Table 2. Museum X Compared to Other Art Museums: Sources of Income

Art museums		Museum X
18%	Endowment income	——
22%	Earned income	43%
6	Admissions	5
1	Concerts/lectures/films	——
6	Store	9
1	Restaurant	——
1	Tuition	——
1	Participation fees	25
2	Special events	——
4	Other earned	4
60%	Contributed income	57%
18	Individuals	20
9	Corporations	1
9	Foundations	13
18	Government	23
6	Events	——
100%	Total	100%

These data can be used to compare financial performance, allocation of resources, staffing levels, funding sources, and the size of endowments and other long-term assets.

The parameters selected to compare should depend, in great measure, on the results of the environmental analysis (e.g., Is an endowment crucial in this industry? Is developing a base of corporate support important?).

For example, Museum X has an income distribution that differed markedly from other art museums.

This analysis reveals Museum X's reliance on renting its exhibitions to other museums and on government funding. Given the precarious nature of government funding and the increasing competition for exhibition rentals, Museum X faces the challenge of building its contributed income base.

THE CYCLE AUDIT

These analyses provide important high-level insight into the strengths and weaknesses of an organization. But more depth is required to isolate many issues that must be addressed in the strategic plan.

A simple model of successful arts organizations, called the Cycle, helps organize this evaluation.The Cycle is a theory of organizational activity that prioritizes investment in great art.

Regardless of art form, geography, or size, thriving arts organizations hold several core characteristics in common:

- Their programming is bold, mission driven, and balanced;
- They aggressively market that programming, as well as the institution behind it;
- The resulting visibility produces a swell of interest and enthusiasm among a "family" of ticket buyers, students, board members, donors, funders, and volunteers;

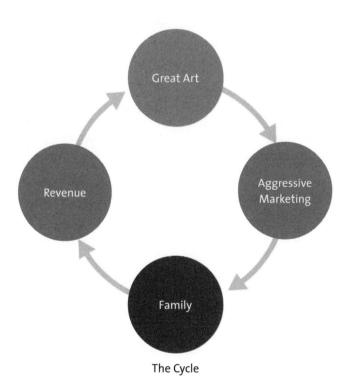

The Cycle

- They make it easy and enjoyable for that family to get more involved by contributing money, time, or connections; and
- They reinvest revenue produced by that family in even bolder programming that, when marketed well, entices an ever-larger and more diverse, generous, and connected family.

When this repeats year after year, all stakeholders—staff, board, and family—sense that they are part of a strong, successful enterprise, and they grow more generous and productive. Their organizations grow incrementally, donor by donor, and slowly build and maintain artistic and financial health.

The cycle describes the work of successful organizations of all types and sizes, urban and rural, and in the United States and abroad. Institute leadership and staff see it not only in performing and presenting organizations but also in museums, arts schools, and other nonprofit endeavors such as service organizations, historical societies, public libraries, university programs, advocacy organizations, botanical gardens, and zoos. Indeed, any nonprofit organization that must fundraise to support its work can benefit from these principles.

The Cycle suggests a list of generic questions provided below that should serve as a useful guide in creating a strong internal audit.

Programming

The mission of every arts organization focuses most closely on programs and services. It is essential that an honest appraisal of program quality and effectiveness lead off an internal analysis.

- What is the nature of the programs offered by the organization?
- Who is served by each program?
- How strong is each program?
- How well is the company received by its audience at home? On tour?
- How well is the company received by critics?
- How does this compare with the peer companies?
- How could each program be improved?
- How much does each program cost?
- How does this compare with the peer companies?
- How are these costs split between personnel and other categories?

- Who is the dominant artistic force? Is this person a visionary?
- What are the backgrounds of the artists/performers/curators?
- Is there a succession plan in place for artistic management?

Education/Outreach

Education and outreach programming is central to the missions of numerous organizations. These arts organizations have a true commitment to their communities; others pursue educational programming because they believe this improves their image with funders. It is becoming increasingly difficult to "fool" funders into believing that superficial efforts deserve serious funding.

- What educational programs are in place?
- Who are target participants?
- How deep is the engagement with participants?
- Is there a specific outreach goal?
- Is there an explicit outreach strategy?
- What are the elements of the outreach activities?
- What internal or external expertise is drawn upon to guide the development of education and outreach programming?

Marketing

The Cycle suggests the importance of visibility for building earned income *and* contributed revenue. Inadequate earned income frequently results from a marketing problem. Price can also be a determining factor. Several major dance companies, for example, have very high name recognition but low levels of earned income; the cost of presenting these companies outstrips the audience's ability to pay for them. Even "famous" organizations can have a visibility deficit. Visibility does not simply imply name recognition; visibility comes to those organizations that are doing exciting things and attract ongoing attention. Understanding the resources that build visibility is central to a strong internal analysis.

- How visible is the organization at home, regionally, nationally, and internationally?
- Which approaches to marketing have been tried?
- Which of these have been the most effective?

- Which are the most cost effective?
- Are the online marketing activities of the organization as potent as necessary?
- How many names are on the email list? Is this sufficient?
- Is return on investment measured for all marketing expenditures?
- What percentage of earned income is spent on marketing?
- How does this compare with the peer companies?
- How strong is the marketing staff?
- How well do you understand the demographics of your audience?
- How have audience demographics changed?
- What is the size/characteristics of your potential audience?
- When was the last time the audience was surveyed?
- What does the audience want to see/hear?
- Is there a strong institutional marketing campaign?
- Are major institutional marketing moments spread across the year?
- Does the organization place a spotlight on all facets of its activities?

Development

Few arts organizations are completely satisfied with their fund-raising activities; the feeling that there is always "more money out there," and a compelling need for that money, drives most organizations to evaluate their development efforts closely. In fact, organizations typically devote more attention to their development efforts than to other operations when performing internal analysis.

Evaluating both the portion of the total budget covered by contributed income and the relative importance of each revenue source is an essential part of this analysis. Comparing these statistics to peer companies, and to the industry as a whole, can be very instructive.

Many organizations of color, for example, tend to receive a higher proportion of funding from government and foundations than from corporate and individual donors. While there is nothing "wrong" with this distribution, it does raise some important questions about the security of government funding, the ability to attract additional foundation funding, and the need for added visibility to build corporate and individual gifts.

- How has marketing strength/weakness affected the fund-raising effort?
- How are contributed funds distributed among individual, corporate, foundation, and government donors?
- How do these percentages compare with peer companies?
- Why do these differences exist?
- How much revenue comes from support groups (e.g., guilds)?
- Which approaches to fund-raising have been tried?
- Which have proved to be effective?
- What percentage of revenue must come from development efforts?
- How has this percentage changed?
- How does this ratio compare with peer companies?
- How has the development effort grown?
- What is the dispersion of the gifts? (Starting with the largest donors, how many does it take to add up to 25 percent of total fund-raising? 50 percent? 75 percent?)
- Has a special capital campaign been mounted recently?
- How effective was it?
- How did the special campaign affect the annual campaign?
- How strong is the development staff?
- How active is the board in fund-raising?
- How much does the board contribute?

Board of Directors

For most organizations, the board of directors represents the most important fund-raising tool. An effective board is a requirement for long-term, consistent success in the arts.

- Who is on the board?
- What are the board members' backgrounds?
- Is the board strong enough to provide leadership and philanthropic support?
- What skills are present on the board?
- What skills are lacking on the board?
- What are the requirements of board membership?
- How does this compare with peer companies?

- Are all of the communities served represented?
- How does your board compare with other boards in your city?
- How involved is the board in operations?
- How involved is the board in fund-raising?
- How effective is the board in fund-raising?
- What board committees have been created?
- Do they meet?
- Are they effective?
- How important is the executive committee?
- How are members of the executive committee selected?
- Is there a succession plan in place?

Staffing

While the strength of the board is a central determinant of any organi-zation's success, the professional staff in all but the smallest arts groups is responsible for implementing major initiatives. A careful analysis of the staff size, structure, and quality is a key element of any internal analysis.

- How large is the administrative staff?
- How does this compare with the peer companies?
- How do salary levels compare with industry averages?
- How is the staff organized?
- Are roles and responsibilities explicit?
- How rapid is turnover? Why?
- What is the total cost of administration?
- How does this compare with peer companies?
- What is the experience level of the staff?

Facility

The development of many institutions is limited by the physical facili-ties available to them. A museum's exhibition space, a dance company's studios, all organizations' office space, and so forth, are central assets that, in many instances, define the boundaries of growth.

- Are the performance/exhibition/public programming facilities adequate?
- What needed facility is lacking?

- Is rehearsal space/collection storage space adequate?
- Does the physical facility limit achievement of the mission?
- Is office space satisfactory?
- How expensive is the facility to own/rent/maintain?

Technology

It is increasingly important for arts organizations to address how they use technology.

- Does the organization have the technology expertise required to build systems that help the organization operate efficiently, market effectively, and maintain communication with audience members and visitors?
- Does it have the computer equipment it needs?
- Does it have expertise in using technology to advance the marketing effort?
- Does it have web development skills?
- Are social networking activities sufficient?
- Has technology been used in art-making? In education?
- Has technology been used to maintain relationships with audience members and students?

Financial Performance

A substantial portion of the internal analysis should be devoted to understanding the financial structure and strength of the organization. Invariably, a considerable portion of the plan will deal with methods for building financial strength; a clear picture of the current position is essential. Financial analysis will also indicate how the organization's resources are used. Comparing this analysis to industry averages or to peer organizations will raise important questions regarding the appropriateness of current resource allocation decisions.

- How does its fiscal strength compare with peer companies?
- In which areas does the organization overspend?
- In which areas does it underspend?
- How does revenue compare with expenses? How has this changed?
- Does the company have an endowment?

- Does the company have a working capital reserve?
- How liquid is the company?
- How much debt does the company carry?
- How has this level changed?
- Does the company have an accumulated deficit?
- How has it changed?
- Does the company have a cash balance?
- How large is the company's line of credit?
- At which times of the year is cash flow a major problem?
- Are these times predictable? Manageable?

Support Groups/Volunteers

Many arts organizations have extra-board groups of supporters who raise funds, volunteer their services, and serve as champions for the organization. It is becoming increasingly difficult to find and motivate volunteers as more and more people work outside the home. Yet a strong volunteer corps can have a profound impact on the organization.

- Does the organization have a guild or other support group?
- What is its charter?
- How much money is raised by the group?
- How does this compare with peer companies?
- How much staff effort is required to manage the group?
- Does the company have an active corps of volunteers?
- How effective are these volunteers?
- Could additional volunteers be used effectively?
- How are volunteers solicited? Managed? Rewarded?

Summary

Once again, it is essential to stress that these questions are simply meant to guide the internal analysis process; they do not address every issue that will face every arts organization, especially those in unusual situations.

In fact, the answers to these and other questions do not comprise the internal analysis. Rather, the insights gained from analyzing the answers should generate a list of strategic issues to address in the plan. In completing an internal analysis, it is important to prioritize these concerns.

The key strategic issues will usually relate to the elements of the Cycle. Office furnishings are rarely an industry success factor, thus they are not likely to be of strategic importance (although a lack of office space may be an important tactical issue). However, the lack of strong fund-raising skills, inadequate attendance, or boring art will be of strategic concern.

A list of major issues can direct the remainder of the planning process. Indeed, the strategizing process is simply a matter of "solving" the issues raised in the external and internal analyses in an integrated manner. This implies that the list must be complete, honest, and accurate, or the entire plan will be ineffective. If issues arise during the strategizing process that were not revealed during the external and internal analyses, these analyses were not completed in a comprehensive manner and must be revisited. A weak internal analysis threatens the integrity of the plan; a solid internal analysis, coupled with a revealing environmental analysis, provides a strong foundation for creative strategy development.

PART 3 Strategizing

5

The internal analysis reveals those areas of concern that must be addressed in the strategy section of the plan. Since programming lies at the heart of the mission of every arts organization, every plan for every arts organization must include a discussion of future artistic and educational programming and needs; this provides the motivation for the remaining sections of the plan.

Many artists are suspicious of efforts to include specific programming plans in a strategic plan. They fear that they will be locked into this programming and will lose their prerogative to change their minds. By no means is planning meant to limit artistic initiative. On the contrary, the goal is to understand the anticipated artistic initiatives well enough to be able to accrue the resources needed to support them. If an arts organization plans to mount expensive and esoteric productions, there are obvious marketing and funding implications: Will a unique marketing approach be needed? Must the organization expect to lose money? Is special underwriting required? Is it available? Are there identifiable donors who may be attracted to this work? The questions must be answered explicitly and unambiguously, so that the organization is not left without the audience it hopes to reach and the funding it requires to continue to produce good work. In fact, too many arts organizations develop strategic plans that include detailed marketing and fund-raising strategies but barely touch artistic plans; it is impossible to imagine how one can market or raise funds if one does not know the works that are going to be performed!

In developing an artistic plan, it is essential to understand the needs of the artists. This is not a simple task. When one asks creative people about their requirements, one frequently receives a very long list. Artists are visionaries, and their visions are typically not constrained by budgets and cash flow considerations. The challenge to the planner is to work with the artists to prioritize their needs. It is not the role of the planner to second-guess the artists. The planner must simply understand the artists' requirements and develop alternative scenarios for meeting them.

If a choreographer hopes to use more dancers, the plan must address this need but in a time frame that allows the organization to function in a fiscally responsible manner. Explaining to the choreographer the implications of the increased costs of adding dancers and identifying those projects that may have to be sacrificed to afford the additions help the artists set their own priorities. It is dangerous when administrators become the decision makers on artistic matters.

While most major opera companies and museums plan their major projects three, four or five years in advance, most other arts organizations plan their art less than two years in advance. This limits artistic quality, marketing opportunities, fund-raising, and touring.

Almost every arts organization should be able to list *major* projects for the next four or five years and complete artistic plans for the next two years. This is vital, since longer-term artistic plans do the following:

- Give the time necessary to plan major projects. If the only projects planned are for the next six to eighteen months, it is difficult to mount the large-scale, transformational projects that bring new attention, audience, and donors to the organization.
- Make it easier to engage important guest artists who may not be available in the near term. Many arts leaders believe, wrongly, that they cannot engage major arts celebrities. Most often, their advances are rejected if they expect the artist to have time in the coming year. Giving an artist a far longer time frame is often key to engaging them.
- Enable joint ventures with major media outlets to create important marketing opportunities; while most arts-related stories are not "sold" far in advance, the longer, more potent magazine, television, and newspaper stories can take months or years to organize.
- Provide the time to identify and cultivate the donors who might be most interested in a specific project. It is far more effective to cultivate individuals or institutions with a deep interest in a particular project than to continuously return to the same set of donors to fund every major project. If one has several years to identify a set of logical funders, and to cultivate them, one is far more likely to receive major underwriting.
- Give tour presenters the information they need to plan in advance.

Table 3. Five-Year Artistic Plan Chart

	2018	*2019*	*2020*	*2021*	*2022*
Program area					
Program area					
Program area					
Program area					
Program area					

Many presenters want to know the specific works an organization will mount before booking a tour date.

- Provide the data required to complete pro forma budgets in advance. Planning programming in advance allows the organization to create pro forma production budgets that indicate if the planned programming is affordable.

In 2009, for example, the Kennedy Center mounted a major festival of Arab culture. It took five years to identify the performers who would best represent the diversity of Arab culture, to create a major marketing program that attracted an audience (many of whom had little knowledge of Arab culture), and to find the funding for this ambitious undertaking. Since the staff of the center had five years to address these concerns, the Arabesque Festival was immensely successful critically, with audiences and financially.

A simple chart that reveals artistic plans over a five-year period helps communicate the artistic plans to all members of the organization required to assist with implementation.

Many artistic directors will be uncomfortable sharing this information at first; they may not have made firm decisions about future projects or may be concerned that revealing their plans will allow other arts organizations to steal their ideas. The planning committee must assure the artistic leader that they recognize that plans can change; in particular, individual repertory works or exhibition concepts can and undoubtedly will change over time. But committing to the largest, most ambitious projects in advance allows the organization to do the longer-term marketing and fund-raising planning that most often results in success.

The planning committee must be free to review the plans with the artistic leader and to give honest, but supportive, feedback on the plan *as a whole*. Is it exciting enough? Does it fully address the mission of the organization? Would collaborations with other institutions be helpful in making the projects more robust? The Cycle suggests that without robust artistic plans, it is impossible to build a healthy, sustainable organization.

Other aspects of the artistic plan may include discussions of facilities; touring; broadcasting; production; and museum publications, public programs, and collections.

FACILITIES

While most arts organizations treat their primary venue as a "given" during the planning process, some artists and administrators wish to change the venue for their performances and exhibitions. Constructing a new facility must be considered carefully, particularly given the high costs of construction and management time and the need to raise capital funds in advance.

Other artists rent facilities that are either too expensive or not sufficient. The decision to move must be made with great forethought. A serious marketing effort aimed at educating audiences about the new location must precede the move, especially if the new facility is larger than the current one. If the new theater is empty, the audience will not enjoy the performance, nor will the artists feel appreciated.

TOURING

Touring is a necessity for many types of arts organizations. For most dance companies, touring is essential, since few companies can perform in their home theaters often enough to meet artistic and financial targets. A few theater companies tour, although the availability of theater in most communities limits the interest in paying tour fees apart from the most popular Broadway musicals. Opera companies tour infrequently, given the high costs. Many symphony orchestras tour, yet the cost frequently exceeds revenue and major underwriting is essential.

Tour dates have become substantially more difficult to book, since many touring subsidies have vanished and the presenters that engage arts groups have suffered from the same economic and funding difficulties as producing organizations. University presenters, important constituents of the presenting community, are under increasing pressure to reduce expenditures and to increase revenue as their parent institutions face budget cuts.

This forces presenters to reduce the number of performances and to book companies on the basis of financial returns. The most visible companies, especially those with lower fees, are a favorite, since they will certainly sell well. The newest organizations may not sell many tickets, but the fees are typically low. Many midsized companies have suffered the most in this environment, with fees so high they are not covered by ticket sales given a modest reputation.

Museum exhibitions tour very frequently, since the cost of creating an exhibition is so large relative to the cost of moving and remounting it. The importance of tour revenue, however, differs substantially between museums.

BROADCASTING

While only a modest number of productions are broadcast on radio and television, an increasing number are now broadcast on the internet. Some organizations look at these broadcasts as a revenue stream, while others are looking to expand the number of people they can serve. Organizations planning to broadcast online must ensure they have the union agreements necessary to do so. And as with all online activities, a careful marketing plan must be developed that attracts viewers, especially as the number of online options increases.

PRODUCTION

The artistic plan must also address the needs of the production staff for performing arts organizations, and the curators, registrars, archivists, and conservators in museums. Requirements for additional personnel, new equipment, and new policies should be addressed.

Frequently, as an organization matures, the growth in production spending outpaces that of artistic expenditures. This growth, however, must be controlled, and the staff must set priorities carefully. Is the new lighting board more important than a new work? Should the cataloging of a collection take priority over a special exhibition? The institutional planning process can proceed only when the artistic leadership has made these decisions.

MUSEUM PUBLICATIONS, PUBLIC PROGRAMS, AND COLLECTIONS

Museums must also make explicit plans regarding catalog (and other) publishing, public programs, and collection development. Publishing is a major expense for many museums. Exhibition catalogs represent permanent documentation, preserving much of the scholarly thinking upon which the exhibition is based. The importance of this written record is unquestioned. The way the catalog is produced, however, as well as the number of copies and the distribution channels employed, must be carefully considered, particularly as technology changes.

Public programs give museums an opportunity to create performances, lectures, and symposia that complement their exhibition programs, while also creating high-profile moments that attract new family members. Museums have been increasing the scope and reach of their public programs, by mounting sophisticated dance performances, multimedia engagements, and social events. Planning for these is not different than planning the activities of a performing arts institution; the longer the lead time, the more opportunity there is to create a program that consistently engages audiences and attracts underwriting.

Plans for collection acquisitions must also be explicitly delineated. The priority given to building the collection will vary depending upon the organization's mission. The cost of acquiring today is so great that every collecting museum must develop clear priorities and a strategy for attracting gifts of collection items as well as purchasing funds and endowments. The time and energy devoted to these activities will clearly compete with the efforts to raise operating funding and endowments. Whether this is a good trade-off or not will depend on the artistic vision and the fiscal situation of the institution.

Everyone reading an artistic plan must be prepared to see the specific elements of that plan change as new opportunities arise. The challenge of entrepreneurial planning, described in the introduction to this book, is nowhere as evident as in the artistic planning for an arts organization.

ARTISTIC PLANNING ISSUES

Each of the following issues should be addressed in the artistic plan:

- What productions (exhibitions) are planned over the next five years?
- How do these productions serve the mission of the organization?
- What message does the slate of productions convey to the public about the mission?
- To what extent will each production appeal to the public?
- To what extent will each production appeal to funders?
- What is the cost of each production?
- Will sufficient earned and unearned income be available to underwrite these costs?
- Where will the productions be mounted?
- Does any production have unusual technical or artistic requirements?
- Will any production feature guest artists of great celebrity?
- Are there opportunities for collaborations with other artistic or educational institutions?
- What impact will this have on cost, ticket prices, marketing strategy, and fund-raising strategy?
- Will any production/exhibition tour?
- Will the touring productions appeal to presenters?
- To what extent will earned income cover touring costs?
- Will additional funding be necessary to cover touring expenses?
- Are there plans to broadcast on radio, television, or the internet?
- Is the venue good enough?
- Is the venue affordable?
- Do any of the planned projects have unusual production requirements?

EDUCATIONAL PROGRAMMING

6

Many arts organizations feel a deep commitment to building the next generation of art lovers and creative artists. Their mission statements clearly and explicitly attest to this commitment. Other arts organizations are feeling pressure from corporate, foundation, and government funders to mount educational programming for underserved audiences and, to a lesser extent, to train talented young artists without the resources to pursue arts training on their own. For both types of organizations, there is an increasing focus on developing and implementing education and training programs.

When developing education and outreach plans, the organization must delineate its goals. Is the purpose to expose underserved audiences to the art form, to use the art form as a method of building character, to use the art form to reinforce academic subjects, or to train young professionals? This decision will affect the design of the outreach programming.

EXPOSURE

Many arts organizations develop outreach programming meant to expose the uninitiated to the beauty of the art form. Of course, the first step is to select the target of these outreach efforts. Some arts institutions focus exclusively on children, others on selected communities, senior citizens, or even prisoners. This selection must depend on the mission of the organization and the availability of funding. These programs are crucial, since most public school districts have cut back substantially on arts programming and many have been forced to abandon arts programming altogether.

Performing arts organizations that rely on touring are under increasing pressure to provide more outreach services while residing in tour cities. The local funders want to know that something was left behind when the company leaves for the next tour city. In-school programs and children's performances are therefore becoming routine for many touring companies.

Ideally, the programs developed for this audience would be coordinated with other, similar offerings so that arts education would be pursued in a consistent manner. At present, many students receive a mixed bag of programs that are not integrated into any meaningful curriculum.

One must question, for example, the lasting impact of the traditional method of exposing young people to the arts: the one-hour assembly program. Repeated exposure for a limited number of students appears to be far more effective than a onetime lecture-demonstration offered to thousands over time. A comprehensive, meaningful strategy will describe target audiences, a set of coordinated programs, and vitally, a methodology for evaluating the true impact of the program.

New 42nd Street in New York City, which operates the New Victory Theater, has created a smart, sophisticated approach to involving students in the arts; while the New Victory Theater provides exposure to thousands of students every year, the organization also provides a pathway for students most interested in theater.

BUILDING CHARACTER

Many arts organizations have developed sophisticated programs that use arts training to instill self-discipline and self-esteem. The joy of improving one's dancing (or painting or acting) skills and developing the discipline to excel in an art form become central life experiences. Requiring extended exposure, these programs can be quite costly to mount.

Funders have become savvier in differentiating between outreach programs. Underwriting for serious efforts that affect young people is available; substantial funding is no longer available for superficial, poorly designed programs. Of course, receiving funding for any program will depend, in some measure, on the reputation the organization has developed for its education and training programs. The techniques for building visibility apply as much to an outreach program as to a performance or exhibition series.

Ailey Camp, founded by the Kansas City Friends of Alvin Ailey, and now a national program, provides opportunities for preteens to learn to dance; the campers' improvement over the summer leads to increased self-esteem and an appreciation for the discipline of dance.

REINFORCING ACADEMIC LESSONS

Curriculum-based arts-in-education programs use the arts to reinforce academic lessons. Rather than teaching dance for the love of movement, curriculum-based programs might use dance to teach mathematics (by focusing on counting), or use the fine arts to teach science (by using plants and animals as models). The ArtsEdge website, created by the Kennedy Center, for example, provides tools for teachers looking to bring the arts into the academic classroom.

Those organizations without substantial experience in this area need to access pedagogical expertise when developing their programs. Outside experts can also offer invaluable assistance by evaluating the effectiveness of the organization's programs. An independent evaluation that suggests ways of improving effectiveness is essential for new program development. Any serious funder will demand a strong evaluation process. The temptation to design one's own education and outreach programs without this feedback should be resisted. Without the expertise of a trained professional, many outreach programs are ineffective.

TRAINING YOUNG ARTISTS

Many arts organizations sponsor their own schools, especially regional dance companies and theater companies. These schools are intended to train amateur, preprofessional and professional artists, frequently of any age.

Any arts institution that chooses to create a school of music, dance, theater, or visual arts should do so simply because of its role in achieving the organization's mission. One corollary benefit these programs offer is the opportunity to employ retired artists as teachers. For many artists, especially dancers, the length of the performing career is short. Schools, and other education programs, allow retired artists to use their experience to help others while earning a living in the profession.

Apart from some major dance academies, few arts organizations actually earn a profit on their schools. Schools are expensive to operate and time consuming to manage. They require a substantial staff, from registrars to teachers, and business managers to guidance counselors. Schools, especially dance schools, also require a great deal of space. While schools can earn some income, many of the best students will be on scholarship. The challenge is to market the school well enough to attract those who can and should pay for their classes and to use some of this revenue to support the scholarship students.

The difficulty keeping company-sponsored schools solvent suggests that a detailed plan must be developed. The planning process can be based on the same framework described in this book:

- The school's mission must be formulated. Is the school trying to train preprofessional artists or to offer high-quality training to young or adult amateurs?
- An environmental analysis will describe the pressures facing arts academies today and in the future.
- An internal analysis will reveal the strengths and weaknesses of the school.
- A series of strategies addressing artistic plans, marketing and development efforts, staffing levels, and so forth, should be developed.
- A plan for implementing these strategies must be included.
- A forecast of projected financial results for the school should be completed.

If managed well, a school can provide important arts training while offering the potential for earned and contributed income and increased organizational visibility; if managed poorly, a school can be a major drain on resources.

Many arts institutions have designed educational programs that achieve substantial economies of scale. This allows the organization to leverage its efforts and also gives funders the benefit of affecting more people with one gift. For example, some organizations have embarked on teacher training, instructing public school educators in the methods for teaching art in their classrooms. One teacher training program can affect hundreds of students each year. Others have embraced online technology that brings education programming to many times the number of children and adults that traditional in-person programs can.

One method for accessing the funds needed to create larger educational programs is to collaborate with another cultural or educational institution. So many organizations are developing similar programs that combining resources can be a highly efficient approach.

Local public schools, colleges, and family service agencies have resources cultural institutions do not have; collaborations can help meet both institutions' missions and financial objectives. (In many cases, consortia of arts and education institutions are collaborating, often with school districts, to ensure a meaningful number of students are getting a comprehensive set of arts experiences.) Joint ventures also give the arts organization access to the board and donors of another institution and the public endorsement of that institution.

While many organizations are introducing educational programming simply to please major funders, those organizations seriously committed to these endeavors are making a difference. Careful planning of all elements of these programs must be pursued to ensure that the programs are as effective as possible and that the funding covers costs. If arts organizations can find ways to coordinate their efforts, the future of arts attendance and performance will be assured.

EDUCATION AND OUTREACH PLANNING ISSUES

Each of the following issues should be addressed in the education and outreach plan:

- Are any education and outreach programs already being offered?
- Have existing programs been successful?
- Which programs are not reaching their potential?
- Can/should some programs be combined or eliminated?
- Which education and outreach programs are planned?
- What is the purpose of these programs? To expose underserved audiences to the art form? To use the art form as a method of building self-esteem? To use the art form to reinforce academic subjects? To train young professionals?
- How do these programs serve the organization's mission?
- How should this programming be managed and staffed?
- Does the organization have the necessary staff to implement these programs effectively?
- Is there an evaluation and assessment process specified for each program?
- Is each program likely to be attractive to funders?

- What is the possibility for establishing a joint venture with another organization? Would a joint venture enhance the program?
- How can these programs gain more visibility?
- How can technology be employed to increase coverage and reduce expenses?

PROGRAMMATIC MARKETING

7

Once the artistic and educational programming plans of the institution have been completed, one can create a plan for attracting audiences, attendees, and students. These "programmatic" marketing plans must address several questions.

WHAT ARE WE SELLING?

While art institutions have, traditionally, created one approach to marketing all of their programming, the most effective and efficient arts marketers realize that there are differences between the types of programming that should influence the marketing investment made and the techniques employed.

Art that is a very easy sell—accessible programming featuring major stars—requires "informational" marketing; we need only let people know when and where to buy tickets we are likely to sell very well. This does not require a major marketing budget. If we are selling a concert with Yo-Yo Ma or Placido Domingo, for example, emails to our list, website information, social media postings, and maybe a simple, inexpensive direct-mail piece should be sufficient. Selling unusual repertory by unknown artists, however, requires "missionary" marketing; we must convince people why they should want to attend this performance or exhibition. This demands a far more expansive and expensive marketing effort to be effective. Photographs, videos, audio clips, creator biographies, quotations from reviews of past performances, and so on, are all essential when marketing unfamiliar works.

TO WHOM ARE WE SELLING?

Since arts organizations must manage marketing expenses carefully, it is vital to focus on specific, target audiences so that marketing efforts can be streamlined as much as possible. Of course, marketing strategy is a game of odds; we are trying to increase the odds of building our audience within the specified budget. Answering the question To whom are we selling? helps increase the odds that our marketing efforts will be successful.

Most arts organizations have a core audience, a group of individuals who are so passionate about the work that they buy tickets, usually far in advance, without real concern about repertory or casting. When this core audience is very large, other marketing efforts can be minimal.

But for most arts organizations, if this core audience purchases only a modest portion of total tickets available, the central question is, Who else should we target? Too many arts organizations spend most of their marketing dollars targeting the core audience. This is not a good use of resources, since this group is already likely to buy. Too many other arts organizations spread marketing dollars across a very broad set of people and geography; the amount of marketing hitting any one person or subgroup is, therefore, minimal.

Since marketing messages must be received numerous times to be effective, it is far more advantageous to focus marketing efforts on what can be termed the "marginal buyer." The marginal buyer is someone who very well might buy a ticket, or might instead watch an online arts presentation or go out to dinner or enjoy another arts experience. Identifying and focusing efforts on these marginal buyers is the most effective way to deploy marketing resources, because the odds that a marginal buyer will respond positively to a marketing message are so much greater.

WHAT IS THE PACKAGE WE ARE SELLING?

There are many different ways to package tickets for sale. The simplest delineation is between tickets sold in a subscription package and those sold individually.

Those organizations that perform for a substantial length of time in any one city have the opportunity to develop subscription offers of two or more performances. While subscription rates are falling due to high ticket prices and the complications of scheduling attendance in advance, many organizations have successfully built subscription efforts by offering discounts, great flexibility in selecting performances, and subscriber-only benefits.

A great effort is made to attract subscribers, since they offer three important benefits to arts organizations in addition to providing multiple sales: they help cash flow by securing funds before the season, they reduce the cost of marketing, and they allow the artistic team more flexibility in selecting repertory.

Just as magazine subscriptions allow the publisher the luxury of collecting revenue before the costs of publication are incurred, so too do subscriptions help arts organizations by producing cash prior to the start of a season. This is frequently the time when cash is most needed, since production and marketing costs are being incurred but no other earned income is available. Many theater companies, for example, survive throughout the summer months on subscription revenue.

Selling a package typically requires a far less expensive marketing effort than selling each ticket individually. A subscription brochure (hard copy or online) and, perhaps, some telemarketing is all that is required for a subscription that may include from two to ten tickets. Selling each of those tickets individually often requires direct mail, advertising (in newspapers, radio, or online), and a social media effort.

Perhaps most important, though more subtle, is the impact on artistic flexibility. When a theater, dance, or opera company knows that its subscribers will purchase a substantial portion of its house, it has the option to offer more innovative or risky programming as part of the season because so many seats will be presold to subscribers. When one relies very heavily on single ticket sales, esoteric repertory can be a bigger financial challenge.

Subscriptions also reduce the impact of negative reviews on ticket sales. Those arts organizations without major subscription efforts are vulnerable to poor critical response. Those with strong subscription efforts are protected to the extent that their seats are presold.

It is difficult to sell subscriptions for arts organizations with short, compact seasons, since most people will not attend the same type of performance more than once in a short time frame. (There are always some who are so devoted to an organization or an art form that they will return many times even in one week, but these people will find the performances anyway and do not require a great deal of marketing!)

While subscription rates have fallen over the past fifty years, it is a mistake to take subscribers for granted. Indeed, each subscriber is an important asset. Great care should be taken to maintain a "relationship" with each subscriber. Calling or writing to each one during the year, or inviting subscribers to midseason cocktail receptions or season announcements to strengthen this relationship is a good way to increase the odds of a subscription renewal.

Since subscriptions have fallen, single ticket sales now represent the majority of earned income for most performing arts organizations. Yet they are also the most expensive to market and are the least secure sales, affected by poor reviews and bad weather.

Organizations that sell a large quantity of single tickets must wait until the end of the season to know their earned income. This means that a substantial in-season marketing effort will be essential to ensure strong sales. (Organizations that have strong preseason-subscription, group and single ticket sales have the option of reducing the amount, and hence the cost, of the in-season campaign.)

One additional key format for packaging tickets is group sales. Group sales can be the best friends of those arts organizations with many empty seats. Unsold seats are the biggest earned-income waste. Unlike in retail sales where old inventory can be sold, even if at discount prices, "dead wood" at a performance is a complete write-off. Once the performance is over the empty seats have no value. In addition to the financial consequences of unsold seats, the negative impact on those audience members in attendance and on performers can be immense. Arts events are more exciting if the house is full. Numerous empty seats can give the impression that the performance is not a good one, that buying tickets in advance is not necessary, and that other people think there are better things to do with their free time and money.

While the most devoted arts patrons will not rely on the judgment of others, the marginal audience member will. (Donors as well will be disappointed to see that the organization they support is not of interest to a larger portion of the community.) Empty houses are the worst enemies of remarketing and must be avoided assiduously.

Group sales fill empty seats quickly. Community groups, congregations, corporate groups, and so forth, are likely candidates for discounted group tickets. Even deep discounts result in some income and help fill the house. The Girl Scouts of America have proved to be a great partner in group sales efforts; local troops can have many thousands of members and volunteers who are happy to participate in arts events at discounted ticket prices.

The power generated by filling empty seats is great. The first time an organization that traditionally suffers from poor attendance sells out, the entire community, including funders, takes notice and everyone is encouraged to buy tickets earlier the next season.

Building a group sales program requires artistic and administrative planning. Groups tend to buy well in advance and will frequently want to know the repertory they will see before committing to the purchase. Personnel must also be dedicated to the effort of creating appropriate direct-mail pieces, following up with telephone calls, completing the sales contract, and meeting the individual needs of each group. Many arts organizations have group sales staff; others use interns. In either case, sincere attention to each group will encourage them to return in the future — a very low cost resale.

One way to increase group sales is to ask corporations to purchase blocks of tickets for the benefit of other not-for-profit organizations they support. For example, tickets for a performance by a symphony could be purchased and contributed to a children's service agency. This way the corporation can contribute to two organizations at once. The agency benefits from the exposure the children get to the concert; the symphony benefits from increased earned income and the service to the community. This offers a good opportunity to build a relationship with a new corporate donor. By providing visibility for that corporation, through signage, program listing, or other methods, it is very possible that increased support may be forthcoming.

AT WHAT PRICE?

Optimal ticket pricing is truly a matter of experimentation. While surveying the prices of peer company tickets can be helpful, and history will usually reveal how much can be charged for seats, as audiences change it becomes difficult to know, for sure, what ticket prices can be charged.

One general observation is critical. Ticket sales for arts events seem to be governed by a kinked demand curve. While one learns in economics class about supply and demand curves, they are typically drawn as straight lines; this implies that the same level of price elasticity exists at any price level for a particular commodity. In other words, increases in prices yield similar decreases in demand no matter where one is along the spectrum of prices.

But observation of arts audiences suggests that the demand curve is actually kinked, meaning that there is far greater price elasticity for lower-price tickets than for higher-price tickets. This suggests that increasing prices for higher price tickets may actually yield a net benefit:

one will sell almost the same number of tickets but at a higher price. On the other hand, raising lower price tickets can actually reduce total revenue, since the number of people willing to buy low-end tickets at the higher price may decline very quickly.

A good ticket price plan must allow for experimentation: Which buyers do not care about prices? Which are very price sensitive? How much can we charge in each section of the house? It takes a willingness to experiment with different pricing schemes to determine what works for your organization.

Many organizations have been increasing their use of dynamic pricing: increasing ticket prices when demand is high and reducing them when demand is low. Successful dynamic pricing programs require very frequent evaluations of sales, enough of a marketing program to convey new ticket prices (especially if they are reduced), and a flexible box office system that can adopt the new prices from one day to the next.

USING WHICH MEDIA?

A great deal of time, energy, and money is devoted to building audiences for arts organizations. Traditionally, arts institutions could rely on a standard set of tools for building audiences: direct mail, paid advertising, posters, press (both advance stories and reviews), and word of mouth were the central techniques used. But as online marketing tools have proliferated, and as traditional methods for reaching audiences have dwindled in importance, the arts marketer has more choices than ever to reach new and returning audiences. The irony is that these choices have made marketing decisions more difficult rather than simpler. How people get their information and what drives them to performances is changing, and despite the amount of study in this area, no one really knows how to build the most effective marketing program now and, especially, in the future. Twenty years ago, the marketing for Kennedy Center performances was dominated by print media, direct mail, and radio advertising. Today, the resources devoted to radio advertising are minimal, print media spending is modest, and marketing campaigns are dominated by online advertising, social media, and a sophisticated email program. Direct mail continues to an important contributor; the bimonthly Kennedy Center magazine is still a favored source of information for many audience members.

Planning for marketing campaigns must include explicit experimentation with available tools and techniques. This does not mean that planning is not essential; rather, some of the specific tactics used will change over time.

Direct Mail

Direct mail has traditionally been one central method for preselling a season to subscribers, groups, and single ticket purchasers. Direct mail has the advantage of giving the marketer access to the home or office with the opportunity to convey a great deal of information at relatively low cost.

Yet the costs of printing and mailing are rising and marketers face the challenge of improving the focus of their direct-mail campaigns. It is not unusual, in fact, for organizations to reduce the number of items mailed substantially, while retaining the same level of revenue by focusing on mailing productivity. While the size of any direct-mail effort will depend upon the size of the organization, its marketing budget, and its earned-income potential, direct-mail efforts must be focused. Organizations that do a good job of keeping track of those who respond to direct-mail pieces are able to increase the efficiency of these efforts.

The design of a direct-mail piece is always the subject of endless discussions among executive directors, artistic directors, marketers, and other interested personnel. Clearly any design of any organizational publication must be consistent with the artistic perspective of the organization. Yet when designing marketing materials, it is also essential to remember that they are meant to capture the marginal sale, since the most loyal audience members will buy tickets anyway.

To the marginal buyer we must convey a reason for purchasing tickets. We must convince them that they want to buy tickets. This form of marketing is more difficult and must influence the design of all marketing materials, including direct-mail pieces. Brochures and other mailers must capture the excitement and beauty of the work. Too often, organizations use images and designs that are beloved by insiders but are not as interesting to the marginal buyer. By "preaching to the choir," we lose the opportunity for marginal sales.

Posters

Many arts organizations have relied upon posters as a major marketing vehicle. This is especially true of organizations with very limited budgets or those whose audiences are confined to a small geographic area (e.g., university campus).

Posters can be a support to an organized marketing effort and, in some communities, have become a primary vehicle for selling the arts. But posters have limited effectiveness for most large arts organizations and should be considered complements to other marketing initiatives. Posters are purely informational, offering very little opportunity for conveying any detailed messages. The name of the organization and the dates and location of the performances are virtually all that anyone can read and remember from a poster. This is typically not enough, even if the design is enticing, to convince a marginal buyer to purchase a ticket.

Print Advertising

For many years, print advertising was the dominant single-ticket marketing technique for many arts organizations. With technological advancements changing the way people get their news and information, print advertising has become a far less potent marketing tool. There are still many arts lovers, to be sure, who enjoy reading their daily newspaper, but far more are now getting news online; this has reduced substantially the budgets allocated to print.

Radio/Television Advertising

Density of coverage is of particular concern when considering an electronic media strategy, since each placement is very expensive. Yet running a radio advertisement only a few times is not likely to have much impact and hardly justifies the production costs. For this reason, broadcast media should only be considered for those organizations that have a substantial advertising budget and can support the purchase of a sizeable quantity of radio or television time. (Radio time, for either advertisements or on-air promotions, can often be traded for tickets to performances, a good way to stretch a marketing budget.)

Telemarketing

Telemarketing has been a very effective method for selling subscriptions and single tickets in numerous markets. Efforts to build telephone sales have been particularly profitable for organizations that are very visible and underwrite sizeable, professional telemarketing campaigns. Amateur efforts predictably do not work as well. Volunteer callers lose interest, the telemarketing scripts are not as effective, and the scale of the effort is too small to earn a substantial return. As with every element of a marketing campaign, it pays to work with talented experts. The costs of running advertisements, printing and mailing brochures, and implementing a telemarketing campaign are large; it is wise to spend some money to ensure that the design of these efforts justifies the implementation cost. As an increasing number of people use cell phones instead of land lines, and have call-screening capability, the success rate of telemarketing efforts has fallen. Many organizations have abandoned use of these efforts entirely.

Websites

Over the past twenty-five years, websites have become a standard tool for marketing tickets. But unlike paid advertising or direct mail, which are proactive marketing tools, websites are more reactive; they require the potential ticket buyer to have made a decision to visit the site. The challenge for most organizations, therefore, is to drive people to the website. While the core audience will be familiar with the web address, marginal buyers must know enough about the organization to want to visit. Websites, therefore, cannot be the only marketing tool employed. They form an important complement to the other marketing tools. Websites must also be designed to encourage repeat visits. If the home page never changes and the information posted is stale, people will not return.

Email Blasts

Emails have become a ubiquitous form of marketing. They allow the organization to present far more information than can be displayed in a direct-mail piece, and they can drive the reader to the website or other venue for actually making a ticket purchase online. Since emails are so potent, organizations are well served to build their email lists. Strategic plans can and should include explicit targets for building the size of the email list. But the proliferation of emails from organizations encourages many recipients to delete emails without opening them. Limiting the number of emails sent from your organization, putting enticing messages in the subject line, and offering discounts with every email blast are all techniques for increasing the open rate for your email blasts.

Social Media

Posting on social media sites is an increasingly popular method for marketing to audiences. The cost is minimal and the outreach can be strong. But social media posts are typically read and processed quickly; the amount of information you can communicate is limited. This suggests that a social media effort must be used to complement other marketing tools. It is essential, as well, to be clear about who you are trying to reach before selecting a social media platform and to ensure that as your target audience moves from platform to platform, your social media efforts migrate as well. For example, while Facebook is the network of choice for many middle-aged people, younger people have moved on to newer platforms.

Online Advertising

Online advertisements are, essentially, a more potent form of posters. They can present a limited amount of information, but for the projects that simply require informational marketing, they can be extremely potent for those organizations with enough budget to purchase them.

On-Site Remarketing

Too many arts organizations ignore the best opportunity for the most focused marketing possible: remarketing to those attending the organization's exhibitions or productions. Whenever possible, marketing for the next season should begin during the current one. Advertisements in programs, signage, and other promotional materials can be the most effective, least costly marketing vehicles.

The smart marketing campaigns match the technique to the nature of the work and the ways target audiences receive information. No matter which basket of marketing tools one uses, it is essential to measure the return on investment (ROI) for each tool to ensure that the marketing effort is as cost efficient as it can be. Too often, arts organizations fail to evaluate which tools are working and which are not. This type of analysis is essential for ensuring that marketing budgets are spent wisely, especially as the way people receive information changes so rapidly.

PROGRAMMATIC MARKETING ISSUES

Each of the following issues should be addressed in the marketing plan:

- What is the most effective way to attract an audience for each production/exhibition?
- Should the organization sell subscriptions?
- To whom should the subscription campaign be aimed?
- How should the performances be packaged?
- Should the organization offer a subscription discount?
- Should the organization offer subscription benefits?
- Whom should the organization target for group sales?
- Which marketing methods will be most effective for selling single tickets?
- Is direct mail a cost-effective option?
- How will the organization build a mailing list?
- Do the mailers accurately convey the organization's artistic perspective?
- How will the effectiveness of each mailing list be tracked?
- Would posters be effective?
- What information should the posters convey?
- When and where should the posters be hung?
- What is the budget for the print campaign?
- How important is the size of each advertisement?
- How often should advertisements be placed?
- Where should the advertisements be placed?
- Is electronic advertising appropriate for the organization?
- Can the organization afford electronic advertising?
- Is telemarketing an effective marketing method for the organization?
- Can the organization afford to implement a proper telemarketing campaign?
- Who is the target audience?
- Do the organization's email blasts have a high open rate?
- Which marketing vehicles are going to be employed for the organization's on-site remarketing?
- Does the website encourage repeat visits?

- Have each of the organization's marketing elements been scheduled to achieve maximum effectiveness?
- Is the social media campaign changing to reflect the use of new platforms by target audiences?
- Is the organization measuring ROI on all marketing expenditures?

8

While programmatic marketing is aimed at building audiences, visitors, and student enrollment, institutional marketing attempts to educate potential ticket buyers and, especially, donors about the excitement that comes from participating with the organization.

Strong programming and aggressive institutional marketing are prerequisites for establishing a sustainable, successful fund-raising effort. Strong institutional marketing also assists with

- attracting new volunteers and, especially, new board members;
- reducing the cost of programmatic marketing efforts;
- building subscription efforts; and
- encouraging board members to participate actively in fund-raising.

A comprehensive institutional marketing plan addresses the following questions.

WHAT IMAGE ARE WE TRYING TO PROJECT?

As with any marketing campaign, a crucial first step is to be clear about the message one is trying to convey to the public. This is more complicated than it might at first seem. Programmatic marketing campaigns are intended to create excitement for specific performances, exhibitions, classes, or events. Yet many arts institutions do work for which there is little or no earned income available. Institutional marketing campaigns are intended to project a more complete image of the organization; community engagement activities, for example, rarely receive much programmatic marketing attention but can often play a pivotal role in creating a rounded, complete, and compelling picture of the organization as a whole.

Smart institutional marketing efforts, therefore, are based on an explicit evaluation of the many aspects and messages the organization wants to portray: our art is amazing, our educational programs are important, our touring activity makes us ambassadors to the world, our financial health is strong, our training activities are creating the next generation of artists, our internship program exposes underserved audiences to new job opportunities, we are the most fun place in town, we are the most important not-for-profit in the region, and so forth. No organization can convey all of these messages; the institutional marketing plan has to delineate which are key for one's organization. But focusing on only one of these messages may not engage a broad enough spectrum of the community. The Los Angeles Philharmonic has grown to become the largest orchestra in the United States, in part because its recently departed president, Debora Borda, created a series of institutional marketing moments—from community outreach activities to ambitious semi-staged opera performances and new uses for technology—that excited and attracted a large number of audience members and donors.

WHAT TOOLS WILL WE EMPLOY IN OUR INSTITUTIONAL MARKETING EFFORTS?

The institutional marketing campaign is a series of moments that, taken together, present an impression about the organization. Before one can decide which tools to employ, one must assess the "assets" of the organization. Key questions to ask include the following:

- What major productions or exhibitions are we mounting in the coming years?
- Which important artists will be working with us?
- Are there celebrities we plan to use as emcees or hosts for our various events?
- Is there a major political, sports, or corporate event happening in our region that we could participate in?
- Do we have a major anniversary coming up? If so, what events are planned?
- Can we do an exhibition about our history and contributions to the community?
- Is there major positive financial news we can announce?
- Did we receive a major new grant?
- Is there an important new artistic or executive leader to announce?

- Are we going to be on television?
- Is there a major joint venture or project we can announce?
- Have we received a major award?
- Have we embraced technology in a new and exciting way?
- Are we building a new building?

For many arts institutions, the answers to these questions will result in a surfeit of events that can populate the institutional marketing campaign. One can imagine the number of institutional marketing moments facing the Art Institute of Chicago; the institution mounts remarkable exhibitions, public programs, and educational programs, and works regularly with artists, educators, and donors of renown. For others, the number of positive answers will be so few that they must invent an institutional marketing moment. Many organizations create a special series of master classes or interviews with important artists; others mount engaging season announcement events or student recitals hosted by an important entertainment, political, or sports star. Very often board members will have links to important people who could be used to populate our special events or knowledge about events happening in town that can be used as the basis for an institutional marketing moment for the organization. When the Royal Opera House in London was closed for renovation, there were few projects that could excite the very people the opera house needed to provide support required to complete the renovation. So its leadership created a "topping out" ceremony when a portion of the renovation was completed; this ceremony provided an opportunity for donors, government officials, and press to celebrate the progress to date and to anticipate the completion of the new facility.

The organization can then mobilize to exploit a series of these assets, ensuring that the people one wants to influence are aware of these activities and can participate.

WHAT IS OUR INSTITUTIONAL MARKETING CALENDAR FOR THE NEXT EIGHTEEN MONTHS?

These institutional marketing moments must then be arranged on a calendar. It is useful to think a year and a half ahead in creating an institutional marketing calendar. Ideally, the moments are not bunched in one time frame but happen periodically throughout the year.

Some moments may happen every year: the annual gala for instance. Others are onetime events that do not reoccur. The latter are the ones that typically have the most impact (surprise is a key element of a truly successful institutional marketing effort), but a healthy mix of both is fine.

What does not work is a calendar so filled with moments that donors, prospect, and even the board members cannot focus on any one event; some prioritization is required. What also does not work is only one moment a year. No matter how large and stunning, one event does not create enough buzz to last a year, particularly in the current environment of daily (hourly?) news stories and special events that claim the attention of the public.

Here are a few important notes about a strong institutional marketing effort:

- Institutional marketing is not classic branding. While branding vehicles (logos, taglines, typeface, stationary design, etc.) can be part of an institutional marketing effort, they cannot be the *only* aspects of it. Most arts institutions do not have the resources to promote logos and tag lines. Institutional marketing efforts are typically a set of impactful events not a set of collateral materials.
- In fact, most institutional marketing efforts are not expensive. While they require staff time (and, sometimes, board time) to implement, they often rely on other organizations, individuals, and the media; the strongest institutional marketing efforts cost very little.
- Not every institutional marketing event requires press attention. Very often, the most potent events influence a handful of people, but if these are the right people, the event can be very effective. Other moments can occur online, influencing thousands of participants over a wide geography.
- Institutional marketing efforts are enhanced when someone is the "face" of the organization. Most often this will be the artistic leader, though some artists are not comfortable in this forward-facing role.
- Lots of little stories are not as potent as one big story. Institutional marketing, like great art, transforms the way a group of people view

the organization. Just as a series of very modestly ambitious artistic programs do not have the same impact as one massive moment, a series of minor mentions about the organization in newsletters or even the press do not equal a major announcement, special event, or project.

Institutional marketing (IM) questions to be answered include the following:

- Does the organization maintain a rolling eighteen-month institutional marketing calendar?
- Are the major IM moments spread throughout the year?
- Is every IM moment a repeat from the year before, or does each year have some special, onetime-only moments?
- What are the major marketing moments for the next eighteen months?
- Is the entire organization aware of these moments?
- Who is responsible for ensuring that the institutional marketing calendar is perpetually updated?
- Are board members actively involved in institutional marketing for the organization?
- Is the institutional marketing effort integrated with the development calendar for maximum impact?

DEVELOPMENT PLANNING

9

One payoff of dynamic artistic and educational programming and an aggressive institutional marketing effort is greater fund-raising success. But success is not guaranteed. A clear development plan is needed.

The impact of institutional marketing techniques on fund-raising results can be great for those organizations that have suffered an extended period of challenge. Changing the conversation from discussions of cash shortfalls, threats to solvency, and restricted activity to focus on achievement, excitement, and fun can impel donors to become more generous and prospects to take a second look at the organization. While a few donors are motivated to help those in great need, a far larger segment of donors is inspired to help organizations that appear vital. When arts organizations produce exciting art and strong institutional marketing programs, they put themselves in position to mount dynamic and productive development campaigns as well.

Plans for these campaigns must explicitly address the following four steps of fund-raising:

1. *Prospecting.* A strong prospect list is the starting point for good fund-raising. But the quality of the list is far more important than its length. Focus on developing a prospect list of one to two hundred names of people, corporations, and foundations that have a strong interest in your work, and people or organizations that have a pattern of giving to similar institutions. It is not critical that each name be capable of making a huge gift, but inclusion suggests that a meaningful gift could be raised. The list of prospects can be gleaned from past givers, givers to other similar organizations (make sure to keep program books of other organizations or photograph their donor walls), articles in the newspaper about new corporations, or individuals who have moved in to the region. But the best source of donor prospect names is from board members; make sure that there is an easy mechanism for board and staff to tell the development staff about people they know or have met who are likely prospects.

This prospect list should be reviewed weekly by staff and monthly with a board development committee to determine who should stay on the list and, more important, to ensure that a strong, tailored cultivation strategy is developed for each prospect.

2. *Cultivation.* Cultivation is the critical second step of fund-raising. The traditional role of cultivation is to allow the prospect to get to know the organization, to appreciate its contributions to the community, and to observe how donors are treated. But it is also vital during the cultivation process for the organization to learn so much about the prospect that it is easy to draft a tailored proposal. One way to learn the best approach to any prospect is to ask, What was your favorite experience giving to an arts institution? The response to this question will invariably provide many clues about what to ask for, how much to ask for, and who should ask.

A good cultivation effort also reveals what might motivate the donor to give. For example, most individual donors give for one of four basic reasons:

a. They love the art. These are the easiest donors to cultivate, since they have a natural reason for supporting the organization.

b. They enjoy meeting famous artists. These donors can be cultivated by introducing them to the artists who are working with the organization.

c. They are looking for prestige. These donors can be cultivated by showing how you recognize and treat major donors.

d. They are looking for a social life. These donors will be impressed by the nature and number of your donor events.

Once one has determined which group or groups the prospect belongs to, it is easier to develop a strong cultivation strategy.

The main goal of cultivation, of course, is to encourage prospects to become more involved with the organization and more knowledgeable about its activities and service to the community. To build involvement means that one has to do more than just send a series of newsletters and emails. These will invariably go unread unless they are connected to events that are more engaging. There are a number of more sophisticated cultivation tools available.

For example, invitations to a backstage tour or to the installation of a major exhibition can be very enticing. Most people appreciate unusual experiences. Bringing prospective donors to a rehearsal can be more exciting than inviting them to a public performance.

A dinner or cocktail reception is an ideal forum for educating prospects about an organization. These need not be "hard sell" fund-raising events but rather enjoyable activities that introduce the prospects to other supporters of the organization. Inviting one or more celebrities (from the corporate, political, entertainment, or arts world) will only help to encourage participation.

Remember, however, that one is hoping to find those individuals who will be interested in providing substantial support for the organization; this will usually be successful only if the art matters to the prospects on some level. For this reason, these social events should be linked to a performance, exhibition, lecture, or other program.

Since most arts organizations do more than produce exhibitions and performances, one has the opportunity to interest those individuals who may care more about education and outreach than about art. Bringing prospective supporters to school programs, community outreach events, or other social service programming can often attract individuals who might not otherwise have an interest.

These prospects should also receive systematic mailings of newsletters, articles, and reviews. Upcoming programming should be marketed with special attention given to major events. The goal of this consistent infusion of information is to create the feeling that the organization is incredibly productive, successful, and important.

For the best prospects, a board or staff member should be assigned to monitor the relationship and to coordinate all contact. While the majority of the work of cultivation will typically fall on the staff, in very small organizations, board members should be asked to manage the entire process. Controlling the level of effort is best accomplished by developing an annual cultivation calendar prior to the beginning of the season. The calendar would include performances or exhibitions (at least one per quarter), major mailings, educational activities, and social events that will be used to cultivate the prospect list. Care should be taken to ensure that the sum of the events reflects accurately the scope of the organization.

If these activities are supported by a successful institutional marketing effort they have an even greater chance of being effective. Many prospects will eventually offer financial contributions, introductions to other donors, and service as volunteers or board members.

A tracking system should be developed. Note the number of responses, the type of events that seem to be of major interest, and the board or staff members who have made contact. Over time, a profile of key interests and contacts will emerge. This information can only help in strengthening future fund-raising solicitations.

Prospects who show absolutely no interest in any activities over an entire season can be removed from the list. But do not remove a prospect too quickly; someone may not show personal interest but may have the power to affect corporate, foundation, or government grants. Your campaign to involve that person may be working without your even knowing it!

Pursuing a successful cultivation campaign requires strong coordination of the marketing and development departments. Typically, the development department will take responsibility for the activity. The marketing department must provide many of the materials and much of the information that will be given to the prospects.

3. *Solicitation.* There are three key questions we need to ask with each solicitation: Who is going to make "the ask"? How much are we asking for? And for which project? An organization must be able to answer these three questions before asking for funds.

- "Who will ask" is perhaps the most important question yet typically gets the least thoughtful examination. The proper solicitor can get far more when the prospect views that solicitor as a friend or peer. The development director or executive director should not make every ask. And yet there are some prospects who truly admire the executive director, for example, and would prefer to give to him or her.

- "How much to ask for" is typically answered either by the giving history of the prospect (to your organization or to another) or by signals the prospect has given during the cultivation process. In fact, the answers to all three questions can typically be answered easily if the cultivation process has been used to get to know the prospect as much as to educate the prospect about the organization. When in doubt, give three funding options to prospects who will typically select the one whose cost is in line with their giving plans.

- "What project should we ask for" should be determined during the cultivation process. We should use the time together to explain the various projects in our longer-term plan to determine which are of most interest to the prospect.

4. *Stewardship.* Good stewardship is the most important stage of the fund-raising process. While it is wonderful to receive gifts from new donors, it is easier to receive large gifts from repeat donors. Those donors who come to believe that participation with the organization is a central and vital part of their lives are typically the ones who make the largest gifts, are there when emergency strikes, are the ones to make initial capital gifts to start campaigns, and are the ones to make large bequests.

Good stewardship means working to maintain an active relationship with the donor between gifts. Good stewardship is more a matter of attitude than of specific techniques. Yes, one can send birthday cards, anniversary gifts, invitations to special events, and so forth. But more important is that the donors feel the organization really knows them and truly cares for their happiness. Some donors want very active involvement with the staff; others are far less demanding of time and attention.

But always saying thank you for gifts, ensuring that the ticketing needs of the donors are met, that they are accommodated in as many ways possible, and that they are always made aware of major organizational news are all essential.

Everyone on the staff and board should be involved in some phase of fund-raising:

- Board members must give personally and solicit their friends, associates, and employers.
- The artistic leadership must convey the vitality and quality of the artistic plans to major donors.
- The administrative leader must provide all participants the information they require to make appropriate solicitations.
- The development staff must coordinate all the efforts of the board and staff, implementing a comprehensive fund-raising campaign.
- The remainder of the staff participates in ad hoc meetings with donors; for example, marketing and production staff will be involved in supporting corporate donors.
- Support groups (guilds, auxiliaries, etc.), with appropriate staff

leadership, can raise funds from donors not otherwise reached by the organization's development efforts.

A carefully crafted development plan that focuses the efforts of all participants and supports an organized pursuit of each prospect invariably leads to substantial fund-raising success.

DEVELOPMENT PROCESS PLANNING ISSUES

Each of the following issues should be addressed in the development plan:

- Has the organization developed a list of solicitation targets?
- How many prospects can the organization effectively service?
- Is the organization's cultivation effort organized and consistent?
- Which events would be effective for cultivation?
- Has a system been developed for tracking each prospect?
- Does the organization maintain a profile on each prospect's key interests and contacts?
- Are the right people involved in soliciting gifts?
- Are solicitors trained to ask?
- Are we doing a good job of stewardship for major donors?

Of course, the way we approach prospects will differ by donor type; foundations, corporations, and individuals all require different cultivation, solicitation, and stewardship strategies.

FOUNDATIONS

There are many charitable foundations that give money to arts organizations. In many respects, raising funds from foundations is the most straightforward. A foundation's purpose is to make grants, and it must do so by law; it might as well give to your organization.

Most foundations are regionally focused, giving primarily to the arts organizations in their home territory. Others are national or even international, supporting important organizations regardless of geography. Making the leap from local to national foundation funding represents a milestone in the history of an arts organization. One of the key benefits of building a position as a leader in one's field is to become eligible for national foundation funding.

All foundations fall somewhere along a continuum from professionally managed with established application procedures to family foundations that distribute money according to purely personal interests. Those foundations without professional staff that give according to the wishes of the family members should really be considered individual givers from a strategic perspective. They act like individual donors even if technically the money comes from a foundation.

Competing for grants from professionally managed foundations has become increasingly competitive as arts organizations try to make up for the loss of government and corporate grants. Success often requires investment of substantial time and effort of extensive cultivation. Any one development officer can produce only a limited number of superior grant applications in any given time period. Therefore, it is imperative to research each foundation carefully to develop a list of the most likely prospects. Giving guidelines will reveal whether your organization has a chance for funding. (When developing any solicitation list, it is helpful to research the donors who have given to your peers. While one always hopes to avoid competition for grants, one knows, at least, that these foundations do support the arts.)

When possible, a meeting with foundation personnel should precede a formal proposal. Fund-raising is really about developing relationships. It is far easier to receive funding when the donor knows you and your organization. (If one of your board members knows and contacts a member of the foundation's board, the chances of having a proposal taken seriously improve. Pass out a list of the board members of the foundations you expect to solicit at your board meetings to identify contacts of this nature.)

When meeting for the first time with foundation executives, *listen* for a description of their giving interests and concerns. This is the best aid you can have in writing a competitive proposal. Taking the time to draft a proposal that addresses the foundation's interests while meeting your organization's needs raises the odds of receiving funding substantially. Even if this proposal is not funded, a relationship with the foundation has been established and future funding is entirely possible, particularly if the foundation executives are impressed with your professionalism. In fact, frequently one may leave an initial meeting without finding an appropriate match between your needs and the foundation's interests. Rather than applying for something that does not fall within the guidelines, waiting for just the right project to materialize will impress the foundation personnel. Again, development means developing productive relationships over a period of time. Simply mailing out hundreds of boilerplate proposals is *not* development.

CORPORATIONS

Unlike foundations, corporations have no legal obligation to contribute to the arts. In fact, fewer corporations are giving for purely philanthropic reasons. Increasingly, grants are tied to the visibility they can create for the corporation. Grants are now frequently made by the marketing staff rather than a contributions or community relations department.

The ability to generate visibility will depend on the importance and accessibility of the project to the audience the corporation is trying to reach. General operating support is not interesting or enticing; it is extremely difficult for most arts organizations to receive large operating gifts from corporations. (In some cities, the dominant corporations take a paternalistic attitude toward local arts institutions and do provide operating funding.)

A special project that creates press and community interest is much more likely to secure corporate underwriting. Therefore, a corporate support plan must include a list of appealing projects and a description of the way visibility will be created for them. The more ways one can build visibility without affecting the artistic product, the better. Signage, website listings program listings, press releases, product placement, stage announcements, and the like, have all been used to promote the sponsor's name.

In addition to the marketing impact of their gifts, many corporations are seeking other benefits from the organizations they support. Reduced-price tickets for their employees, for example, are one way that corporations can justify their contributions. Others use performances as client entertainment opportunities.

Gaining access to corporate executives who develop their firms' marketing strategies is obviously vital to building support. Board members can be very helpful in this endeavor. Many arts organizations have created corporate committees composed of leading executives from the board and the corporate community, each of whom is required to give a modest corporate contribution. More importantly, the members are asked to solicit underwriting from their own corporations and from their colleagues in other firms.

GOVERNMENT AGENCIES

The strategies employed to maximize government funding vary depending on the level of government. While total funding from national government agencies is not increasing, this does not mean that an individual organization that builds a strong record of artistic accomplishment cannot experience growth in funding from federal sources.

State and local government funding depends substantially on the local perspective on the arts. Many states and cities have arts councils that give money in a manner similar to federal agencies. Yet the realities of local politics and the impact of the arts on local economies frequently leave room for more effective lobbying than at the national level. Many arts organizations work diligently to establish strong relationships with local politicians; these organizations frequently benefit substantially from these relationships. Some arts organizations receive long-term substantial support through regional funding—a dedicated tax that supports local arts groups. But winning approval for this is a difficult task in the current antitax environment.

No arts organization can trust that the government funding it receives will be maintained or increased. The tremendous impact of state and local budget cuts in the early 2000s on hundreds of arts organizations is an example of the power of sudden and dramatic cuts in government funding. All arts organizations must work actively to prepare themselves for future cuts of this magnitude by building stronger corporate, foundation, and individual fund-raising efforts and by creating new earned-income opportunities.

INDIVIDUALS

The supply of potential individual donors is unlimited. The challenge is to isolate a group of potential donors and to work effectively to engage them in the activities of the organization. If one can get donors to believe that their happiness is tied to the success of your organization, these donors are likely to give generously.

Some individuals give because of the relationship they enjoy with the solicitor. If a friend, family member, or business associate asks for a contribution, it is difficult to refuse. Still other individual donors believe they can benefit from the reflected glory of the organization. Individual giving will range from low-level memberships to major gifts of substantial size. Membership tends to include the largest number of donors but not the largest portion of contributed revenue. Since the average membership gift is small, arts organizations must be very careful to minimize expenditures on attracting and servicing members.

Many organizations unknowingly lose money on large segments of their membership activities. While the program, in total, may generate net revenue (because the larger membership gifts tend to be quite profitable), the solicitation, mailing, fulfillment, and staff costs of the lower end of the program frequently exceed revenue. In particular, few direct-mail membership campaigns are profitable when one adds in the cost of servicing the new members unless the prospect lists are very focused on the organization's friends. The losses incurred can be justified only if a significant effort to keep members and to move them into higher giving categories is pursued. The introduction of email campaigns and crowd-sourcing has, of course, lowered the cost of fund-raising tremendously.

Midlevel individual givers, those who give from five hundred to five thousand dollars, represent a largely untapped source of revenue for many arts organizations. It is frequently easier and less costly to find one thousand-dollar donor than twenty fifty-dollar donors, yet too many organizations spend more effort on the lower dollar amount because the request seems less daunting. Board members, guild members, and other friends should be able to provide a substantial list of midlevel prospects; working in an organized fashion to cultivate these prospects can be very profitable. The Cycle Model (introduced on page 41) provides a template for the way major donors can become increasingly engaged in the work of the organization.

Typically, access will come through board contacts. Except in unusual circumstances, major donors will support a project that is of personal interest. A useful technique when soliciting a major donor is to be prepared with the five-year menu of projects developed for the artistic plan. The key to successful fund-raising is to listen to the interests of the donor and then to match the donor to the appropriate project. Those solicitors who come to a donor with a sole project have no recourse if it is of little interest.

Culturally specific arts organizations have traditionally had a difficult time finding major individual sponsors. The communities they serve have other giving priorities, and white donors typically support mainstream organizations. The boards and staffs of culturally specific arts organizations, therefore, must work especially hard to build this source of income.

SPECIAL EVENTS

Special events provide a strong vehicle for attracting corporate and individual contributions. Corporations apply the same criteria used to evaluate other arts programming when considering events sponsorship: will the event provide visibility with the right audience? Does the event provide an opportunity for client entertainment? If the event is well planned, both criteria are easily met. Individuals will frequently support a special event if a close associate asks them to help or if the event offers a special entertainment opportunity.

Therefore, the uniqueness of the event and the active participation of the board and the benefit committee will determine success. Most prospects invited to a major special event receive many invitations to similar functions. To compete effectively, one must make an event unique and exciting to a jaded prospect pool. The Kennedy Center Honors, the most profitable annual special event in the arts, is a strong example of the drawing power of glamor and celebrity.

Asking celebrities to participate can be extremely helpful. Many notables from the world of the arts, politics, entertainment, and sports will participate willingly if they believe in the mission of the organization, believe they will have a good time, or expect publicity for attending. Involving celebrities also attracts press interest. Creating visibility, even after the event is over, is useful. It pleases corporate sponsors, and it makes participants feel they were part of something special and newsworthy. This helps sell tickets for future events.

Many arts organizations plan too many events in a given year. While the temptation to raise more is strong, too often an organization that mounts multiple events finds that each one is undersupported and that the total earned is less than the net for one effort that has the full backing of the entire organization.

For any event, however large, the focus must be on the bottom line.

While one hopes all guests will have a wonderful time, costs must be controlled. For many donors, supporting an annual gala is the only way they will help the organization; if a large portion of the ticket price goes to defray the expenses, a great deal of effort results in very little net support.

DEVELOPMENT PLANNING ISSUES

Each of the following issues should be addressed in the development plan:

- Does the organization convey the vitality and quality of its artistic programming to donors?
- Is the effort to solicit foundations adequate?
- Which foundations have given to peer organizations?
- Has each foundation been well researched?
- How can a corporate gifts program be created?
- Has a list of projects likely to appeal to corporate funders been developed?
- Does the organization convey the way in which visibility will be created for the corporate donor?
- Has the organization developed benefits for corporate donors?
- How can positive relationships with local, state, and national government officials be developed?
- Has the organization identified a group of potential individual donors?
- How will the organization engage these individuals in the activities of the organization?
- How can membership be increased?
- Is a direct-mail campaign the most efficient method for reaching your funding audience?
- Has the organization matched the interest of the donor with the appropriate project?
- Have benefit events been planned to maximize both income and visibility?
- How can the board become more involved in fund-raising?
- Does the administrative leadership provide the development staff and board with the information they need to make appropriate solicitations?

- Has the development staff coordinated efforts between board and staff, implementing a comprehensive fund-raising campaign?
- How should the fund-raising program be managed?

SPECIAL CAMPAIGNS

Virtually every arts organization reaches a point in time when it plans a project that cannot be supported by the annual fund-raising drive. Physical expansion, stabilization (reducing the accumulated deficit or establishing or augmenting a working capital reserve or endowment fund), or the pursuit of a major new program will frequently demand more resources than the annual campaign can produce. An arts organization must then contemplate mounting a special campaign.

Before one can even begin to plan for a special campaign, it is essential to develop an absolutely explicit and comprehensive description of the need. Too many organizations conceive of and initiate a special campaign, only to discover midway through the effort that major "hidden costs" were omitted and that the campaign target must be increased. When a physical expansion is planned, for example, organizations frequently omit or underestimate costs of closing during construction, the increased costs of operating the new facility, the cost of running the campaign, or the costs of financing the expansion until pledge payments are received in full. Organizations that do a sloppy job of cost estimation will be evaluated poorly by major donors, at best, and can be financially crippled by a "successful" (but inadequate) campaign, at worst.

When an organization has decided that it needs to mount a campaign, it should consider the range of projects that need to be included. Many organizations planning physical expansions, for example, also include operating endowments in the campaign goal. Arts organizations cannot mount special campaigns very frequently. After any successful campaign, the donors and the staff and board members want to believe they are "finished."

Frequently an ambitious effort will leave the staff, the board, and donors feeling spent. It is difficult enough to fight this postcampaign depression and to get everyone focused on the annual funding needs. If the campaign was inadequately specified, and substantially more money is required, the sense of frustration can be crippling. This is particularly true of organizations that erect new facilities only to find themselves in severe financial straits owing to poor campaign planning. For this reason, all the special needs for the following five or more years should be considered. Broadening the scope of a campaign may also interest donors who are not attracted to the original limited purpose of the campaign.

Without a clear picture of the full cost of the project, it is also impossible to determine the feasibility of the fund-raising effort. Conducting a feasibility study lowers the chances of initiating an unsuccessful campaign. In addition to wasting time and money, unsuccessful campaigns create doubt in the minds of major donors and board members about the management of an arts organization, thereby hampering future major projects.

Feasibility studies can be completed by the organization itself or by a consultant. While internally managed studies are undoubtedly less expensive, an outside consultant may be more objective and can frequently learn more from potential donors. Prospects may be less willing to reveal their true views of the organization and the level at which they might give in a meeting with a staff or board member than in a confidential appointment with an independent consultant.

In fact, a superior feasibility study can teach an organization a great amount about its strengths and weaknesses in dealing with donors, in creating an image of excellence, and in managing its own affairs. These insights can inform the internal analysis in future plans and should be used to strengthen the organization's marketing and annual fund-raising efforts.

Frequently the decision to mount a campaign results from a planning process. One must be careful not to initiate a feasibility study prematurely if the plan also includes strategies for substantially strengthening visibility, the board, donor relations, or other aspects of the organization that will affect the results of the study. It makes sense to delay the study until these other strategies are given a chance to have an impact. Too often, an organization that is planning a major campaign and a concurrent major change in strategy commences a feasibility study that does not accurately measure how donors will feel about the organization after the strategies have been implemented.

The feasibility study may reveal that enough support does exist to launch the campaign; it may indicate that certain changes are required before a campaign can be implemented successfully; or it may suggest that a campaign should be deferred or reduced in scope.

In addition to suggesting whether a campaign has a strong chance of success, a feasibility study will provide a list of prospects who should be solicited early in the campaign. Frequently a strong candidate to serve as the campaign chair will also emerge. The chair will have a major impact on the campaign's success. The ideal chair gives a leadership gift and has the connections and stature to encourage others to give generously.

The most successful campaigns have strong, committed leadership. The chair should be supported by a committee of donors who will work diligently on behalf of the campaign. The committee need not include only board members; in fact, broadening the membership to include corporate and civic leaders can be very effective.

The committee will work with the staff to develop the strategy for the campaign, including the following:

- The expected division of the campaign target into gift categories: Most campaigns receive a few very large or "leadership" gifts, more midsized gifts, and even more smaller gifts.
- Prospect lists for each gift category: Supporting the projected number of gifts that should fall in each category will be a list of realistic prospects for each size gift.
- Solicitation strategies: Different donors will be approached in differing ways. The most important potential donors may require a major presentation; this is obviously not justified for smaller donors.
- Named gift opportunities: Many donors will want to memorialize their gifts by naming a physical structure, endowment fund, staff position, or project for themselves or someone they wish to honor. Creating a strong list of naming opportunities is becoming increasingly important.

The committee will need a coherent statement of the campaign goals. This case statement justifies supporting the institution, relates the needs addressed by the campaign, and reveals the named gift opportunities.

Unless the entire campaign goal is obtained from a very limited number of donors, an organization must be prepared to spend between 3 and

5 percent of the target on campaign expenses. This money is spent publishing the case statement, mounting cultivation events, and hiring additional staff or fund-raising consultants. It is ideal if the organization's development staff, perhaps with some additional temporary employees, can manage the campaign effort. If the time or expertise required is not sufficient, consultants can be hired to manage the campaign. In any case, even if consultants are engaged, it is essential that the relationships formed with campaign prospects include the board or the staff of the organization. An opportunity for future solicitations is wasted if the organization's relationship with the donor ends when the consultants complete their work.

Except in unusual circumstances, donors to the campaign should also become top prospects for the annual campaign. These donors have invested in the future of the arts organization and will probably have a continuing interest in it.

Keeping in touch with campaign donors after the pledge has been received is essential; too many organizations do not have active stewardship programs and ignore the donors who have already committed to the effort in favor of cultivating the next set of prospects. This is a sure method for disengaging the interest of early donors and losing potential future support. All campaign donors should be thanked on an ongoing basis, involved in major events, and treated as important prospects for future gifts.

Keeping campaign donors engaged is also the best way to encourage them to involve their friends in the campaign. One of the best sources of campaign prospects should be the friends and associates of those already giving. Once someone has invested in the campaign, they should be asked to join the campaign committee and to solicit contributions from their personal lists.

Pursuing a major campaign typically requires considerable cultivation of new prospects. Few arts organizations can meet campaign goals solely by soliciting extra contributions from current donors. Producing exciting work and mounting important institutional marketing campaigns are especially important before and during the campaign. The more attention the organization can attract, the greater the chances that new donors will be willing to support its campaign. In other words, the Cycle works!

Board members must be willing to commit their time and their money to the drive. While some organizations must pursue campaigns without the considerable financial support of their boards, most must depend on them for a large portion of the campaign goal. If an organization cannot count on its board to contribute at least one-third of the target, it must have access to major nonboard donors or it must strengthen its board prior to publicizing the campaign. Board gifts are typically pledged before a campaign is formally announced. The reason to delay announcing a campaign until a substantial portion of the target has been pledged is to convince marginal donors that the effort has a high probability of succeeding.

The annual fund-raising campaign must be strong enough to bear the loss of some gifts during and immediately following the campaign. Invariably some donors to a special campaign will reduce their annual gifts while they are making their pledge payments. The organization must calculate an expected loss in the annual effort (the amount of the loss will depend on the overlap between annual donors and campaign donors) and add this amount to the campaign target as a "bridge fund."

Cannibalization of the annual campaign is one reason a serious effort should be made to encourage donors to schedule pledge payments over as short a time period as possible. Obviously short payout schedules also improve cash flow. In fact, when developing an initial campaign cash flow forecast, one must realistically expect that major pledges will be paid out only over a three- to five-year time frame, if not longer. This is an essential consideration, since the cost of money can be quite high for an arts organization. If commitments to spend campaign revenue (on a new building, for example) substantially precede receipt of pledges, the cost of financing to the organization can be significant. Failing to predict pledge payments accurately can result in a campaign target that is inadequate to meet the true project cost.

Arts organizations must also be careful to plan explicitly for the way they intend to inhabit their new facilities. Too many organizations design beautiful new buildings and raise the money needed to erect them and, less frequently, to operate them, without fully accepting the requirements of being a larger institution. The pressure to raise the levels of artistic accomplishment, visibility, financial performance, and staffing can be enormous.

Too few organizations that expand rapidly seize the benefits available to institutions that claim leadership in their fields. Leaders have an easier time attracting press coverage, soliciting major institutional donors, and building audiences. But leadership must be planned for and earned, and many growing institutions fail to do so.

CAMPAIGN PLANNING ISSUES

Each of the following issues should be addressed in the campaign plan:

- Has the organization developed an explicit and comprehensive description of the need?
- Has the organization performed a feasibility study?
- Has a specific campaign target been specified?
- Have campaign costs and transition expenses been adequately budgeted?
- Does sufficient funding exist to meet the goals of the campaign?
- Has the impact of the campaign on the annual fund-raising effort been considered?
- Have prospect lists been created?
- Have solicitation strategies been developed?
- Has the organization created a set of named gift opportunities?
- Does the organization need to hire additional staff or fund-raising consultants?
- Has the organization created a cash flow forecast for the campaign?
- Is the planned artistic programming and institutional marketing sufficient to attract new donors?

10

Board members are the head of the institutional family. We must have a plan for ensuring that the board remains productive and engaged and that its membership evolves as institutional requirements change.

The board of directors (or trustees) of an arts organization is meant to be a leadership and support group that cares deeply for the institution and works diligently to find the resources required to achieve its mission. In fact, next to a strong artistic product, a dynamic, engaged board is the most vital asset of a healthy, robust arts organization.

Yet for many arts executives there is no area of operations that generates more controversy and anxiety than the board. The tension results primarily from the potential of the board, the frequency with which that potential is *not* fully realized, and the power resident in a lay group of volunteers.

While some boards and arts executives enjoy strong working and personal relationships, most troubled arts organizations experience board-staff conflict. The staff virtually always believes that its problems would be solved if the board contributed, or raised, more, and the board frequently blames the institution's problems on staff incompetence. Even in many successful organizations, the conflict between staff and board is palpable.

This tension can be crippling. In today's difficult arts funding environment, the board and the staff must work together; failure to do so inevitably results in the loss of the best board and staff members, substantially reducing the odds of establishing or maintaining organizational health. The strategic plan, therefore, must clearly delineate the roles of the board and must reveal an approach to maximizing its effectiveness while minimizing the potential for conflict with the staff.

Boards serve both legal and nonlegal functions. Legally, the board is responsible for financial oversight, for hiring and firing artistic and administrative leadership, and for setting major policies and strategic plans. The board should also serve, de facto, as ambassadors in the community, as contributors and solicitors of funds and other resources, and as champions of fund-raising events. The board is *not* responsible for making specific operational or artistic decisions. If the board, as a unit, is unhappy with the administrative or artistic direction of the organization, it can remove the artistic or administrative director. Acting on their own, discontented board members can "vote with their feet," choosing to resign from the board and withholding financial support.

The line between active participation and interference is a fine one, particularly with board members who are extremely generous with their time and money. If major donors insist on "poaching," making decisions really the province of the staff, it is difficult and risky to try to rein them in. These powerful contributors must be accommodated and "worked around," as one copes with any other major operational constraint.

In fact, one wants to encourage the interest of board members, while still discouraging unhelpful behavior. Creating engagement on the part of board members is a goal of virtually all arts executives and board leaders. When board members are engaged, they are the most likely to be generous and to work on the organization's behalf by introducing their friends and associates to the organization.

Since boards are agglomerations of personalities, no two are exactly alike. Nor does the board's profile remain unchanged over time. In fact, the nature and roles of the board frequently change in predictable ways as the organization matures. During the institution's formative years, the board tends to be composed of friends of the artistic founder. They are called upon to offer much moral and some financial support. Frequently, these initial directors also act like quasi-staff, helping with numerous staff functions: accounting, legal work, marketing, fund-raising, and even costume sewing on occasion. As the organization matures, however, the demands placed on the board change as well. Typically, operating functions become the province of professional staff, thereby reducing the need for daily board involvement. As the budget and funding requirements grow, board members are called upon to increase their own contributions and to play more active roles in the development campaign. Those individuals who have balanced the books or sewn beautiful costumes may not be in a position to give more money or to solicit more from friends.

This dichotomy between the requirements and the capabilities of the board frequently results in a substantial transition period during which senior board members are replaced by newer ones. This can be a most painful period in the institution's history. Those board members who find themselves losing a role in the organization frequently resent the way their past contributions have become overlooked. While the restructuring must be handled tactfully and thoughtfully, the survival and development of many arts organizations depend, in great measure, on the willingness of the board to reinvent itself. The revitalization of the Alvin Ailey organization, described in chapter 4, was a direct result of this kind of board restructuring.

Those boards with active nominating or governance committees —which evaluate the organization's board needs, evaluate the current members, and identify and nominate new members—are the most likely to handle restructuring effectively. Indeed, evaluating and revitalizing a board should not be a onetime project, nor should it wait for a crisis. The executive staff and board leadership should be working on an ongoing basis to find new board members and to remove those who would better serve the organization in other capacities.

There is no magic formula for finding new board members. The first step is to define clearly the expectations for new members. Is there a requirement for giving or soliciting a specific level of funding? Must members attend board meetings on a regular basis? Is each member expected to serve on a committee? A clear, specific set of guidelines helps potential new board members decide whether they can be successful; it also helps existing members determine whether they should remain on the board. Setting a required level of board giving is a difficult process. Too high a target may result in a very small board; too low a target may dissuade individual members from making major gifts. The correct level depends on the nature of the board, its historic role in supplying funding, and the needs of the institution.

If the board needs strengthening, these requirements should be broadcast to everyone associated with the organization. Corporate and foundation funders, local politicians, old and new board members, major patrons, and so on, will all have ideas for appropriate board candidates. Create a comprehensive list of candidates, and have board and staff leadership visit each candidate ready to explain the organization's needs, its view of board participation, and its plans for the future.

One caveat: There are very few perfect board members with a complete set of required skills, talents, and resources. It is important to develop a board that, as a group, has the requisite assets. Not every member must be wealthy, must fund-raise, must understand the operations of a not-for-profit arts group, or must have a passion for the art form. Some members may be added for their expertise, others for their resources, and others for their link to a community one wishes to serve. The nominating or trusteeship committee must evaluate the current board portfolio of skills and add to it appropriately.

Developing a list of assets needed on the board—the kinds of giving capacities, industry backgrounds, communities represented, skills and talents, and so forth—can produce a picture of an "ideal board" that can serve as a guide for adding new members.

A consistent, coordinated effort to identify and solicit new members invariably results in a systematic improvement in board productivity. While this process should be ongoing, boards that require major overhauls should not add new members one by one. It is far more effective to add new members in bunches. New board members typically learn expected behavior from the more senior members. If the entire board gives in small increments, is uninvolved in fund-raising, and has a tendency to micromanage the staff, a new board member, despite tremendous potential, will learn to mimic this behavior. Adding several new members at one time will increase the chances that the new recruits will bring an energy and a sense of purpose of their own to the board, thereby helping the body to change more rapidly. Having this group of new members meet with senior staff several times before they attend their first board meetings can give them the knowledge they need to be effective board members from day one.

In creating a board, or in reinventing one, it is imperative to remember that the real work typically occurs outside of board meetings. If a board member is willing to allot four hours a month to an organization, and three of them are spent in meetings, there is little time remaining for fund-raising, soliciting new board members, and so on. If an organization has too many board meetings, attendance begins to falter; continuity becomes virtually impossible to achieve. Four to six meetings a year should suffice for most organizations. This allows board members more time to find resources for the institution or to serve on active board committees. (Of course, organizations in crisis may need more frequent meetings.)

Full board meetings can become more efficient if they are characterized by well-thought-out communications by board committees and the staff. Even during periods of crisis, when the full board must tackle a major issue, premeeting discussions between key board and staff should result in proposals for full-board consideration.

Committees can attack an issue in greater depth than can the full board, yielding more effective solutions in a more time-efficient manner. In addition to the governance or nominating committee discussed above, virtually every arts organization should have an executive committee that acts in place of the full board. The executive committee will frequently meet in months when the full board does not. The committee will be composed of the most important contributors, the most knowledgeable board members, and the chairs of the standing committees. Despite the obvious importance of this group, it is vital that the remainder of the board not feel disenfranchised by the unity and power of the executive committee. This is a sure way of eliminating the engagement of the majority of the group.

Every organization also needs a finance committee that is charged with analyzing financial reports, budgets, and audits on behalf of the full board. The finance committee serves as in-house controllers, alerting the full board of impending crises and working with the staff to solve pressing problems. Boards must also have audit committees that function independently of the finance committee to ensure proper accountability.

The formation of other committees will differ by institution. Many boards will have a development committee. It can be dangerous to form a development committee if those board members *not* serving on this committee believe they are absolved of participation in the fund-raising activity. The development committee should be charged with organizing the board's fund-raising efforts, not implementing them. Virtually every board member should participate, in some measure, in accessing resources for the institution.

Other organizations will have a marketing committee. This can also pose problems if the committee's charter is not clearly specified. Too often, board members from the corporate sector believe that the marketing techniques that work for their businesses will be equally successful in the arts. More often than not, this is not true. Corporations spend so much on marketing that they can afford to support speculative programs. As long as the marketing efforts *in total* are successful, it is possible for corporations to take great risks. Arts organizations do not have this luxury. Most allocate small portions of their budgets to marketing but expect a big impact, supporting both earned and unearned income generation. It is dangerous for arts organizations to divert funds from proven marketing methods to new, risky ventures. If a board marketing committee can help to improve existing marketing initiatives or can find additional resources to support new initiatives, they can be very helpful. If they insist that "they can do for the arts organization what they did for their own corporation," they invariably fail.

Indeed marketing committees, development committees, and all board members must appreciate the craft of arts management and the knowledge base and experience of the staff. While there are certainly staff members who do not have the breadth of vision to appreciate some excellent ideas presented by board members, there are many more who can differentiate between a potentially valuable proposal and an inevitably wasteful one. Board members must either trust their senior executives when they reject a board proposal or replace them.

When the board and staff have mutual respect, when the staff works hard to engage the board members in the activities of the organization, and when the board members contribute their time and resources generously, there is little that cannot be accomplished.

BOARD PLANNING ISSUES

Each of the following issues should be addressed in the plan for the board:

- Is the board involved in strategic planning?
- Does the board truly understand the budget?
- Does the board do a good job of engaging and evaluating staff leadership?
- Is the board involved enough in fund-raising?
- Do board members serve as ambassadors for the organization?
- Has the organization defined its ideal board?
- How does the current board membership compare to this ideal?

- How should the board be managed?
- How can board members become more engaged in the activities of the organization?
- Does the organization have appropriate board committees?
- Have the responsibilities for board members been clearly defined and communicated?
- Is there a minimum board requirement for giving or getting gifts?

ORGANIZATIONAL STRUCTURE/STAFFING

11

The adage that structure should follow strategy applies to the organizational structure of an arts organization. Indeed, a key element of the strategy is the way the staff will be organized to accomplish the proposed operating strategies.

If the organizational structure is allowed to determine the strategy, as it does in many institutions, the organization can do little more than maintain its current status. In many instances, unless the structure is changed, the ability of the proposed strategies to create change is severely limited.

This does not mean that the current organization and staffing should be ignored when one is developing a strategic plan, nor that one has absolute flexibility in altering an organization's structure. The institution's historical relationship to particular staff members, union requirements, and other factors will all affect the flexibility the planner has to alter the organizational structure. However, it is frequently true that as strategies are altered, the organizational structure, job descriptions, and even personnel selected to fill important positions must change as well.

There is not one correct organizational structure. As ballet companies mature, they typically have two leaders—one artistic and one administrative. The artistic leader of a ballet company tends to spend so much time in the dance studio that it is essential to have a coequal partner managing the company.

Symphony orchestras also tend to have two leaders, although for major ensembles, the music director is frequently out of town on guest conducting assignments, leaving the executive director or president with greater day-to-day authority than in a dance company. Traditionally, museums and opera companies have had one director who manages both the artistic and administrative sides of the organization but who comes from an arts background. The director is usually supported by a strong administrator.

As the level of sophistication required to market and support any large arts institution has increased, more organizations are experiment-

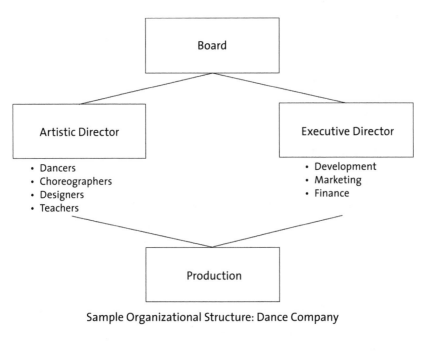

Sample Organizational Structure: Dance Company

Sample Organizational Structure: Museum

ing with the model embraced by dance companies and symphony orchestras.

Yet many boards and staff members of museums and opera companies are skeptical that a dual leadership plan can be effective. They fear that the art will "take a back seat" to the financial status of the organization (or vice versa) and also that the two leaders will be constantly at loggerheads, coming frequently to board leadership to solve an impasse. This structure is not without risk, since it requires a true partnership between the two leaders, each of whom must respect the talents and responsibilities of the other. While it would be ideal to find one individual with a perfect match of artistic vision and administrative skill, such individuals are rare. A partnership model allows the organization to benefit from the best of both worlds.

This suggestion that a new model of management be considered is not a prescription. Many opera companies, museums, and other types of arts organizations will do well with one leader. Nor is it meant to suggest that administrative issues are more important than artistic concerns. Too often, when an arts institution has fiscal problems, the board will decide that the artists are wasteful and that a strong administrator is needed to run the entire organization. The real problem in most of these organizations is not wasteful artists (some of whom do exist) but poor revenue generation capability, stemming from a small family of donors. The problem may call for the addition of a top-level administrative leader, or for bolstering certain staff departments, but it rarely calls for the demotion of the chief artistic personnel.

Indeed, in any management structure, the leadership must be supported by a strong set of functional managers. The number and size of each department will depend upon the size of the budget, what the organization can afford, and the complexity of its operations.

Most arts organizations have a marketing director and a development director, although some institutions place both functions under the leadership of one individual (e.g., director of public affairs). This logical organizational relationship is also a potentially dangerous one. Too frequently, the need for contributions is so great that the director of public affairs becomes a super-development executive and the marketing function is left without a top-level advocate. In the end, this model can result in reduced marketing strength rather than the substantial interplay of marketing and development that was its objective.

The structure of the remaining staff departments depends on the organization. Whether the staff is organized by function (finance, production, etc.), by program, or in some matrix structure should depend on the strategies of the institution and the most effective way to implement them. While most organizations are structured by functional area, many have specific programs that are so discrete that they benefit from separate organizational identities.

The appropriate size of each department also differs by organization. It is helpful to compare the size of one's own departments with those of peer organizations. If similar organizations have three or four development or marketing staff and your organization has only one, you are likely to be at a serious disadvantage. If you have twice the number as your peers, one must question staff productivity and cost effectiveness. How much money is raised on average by each development staff member for your organization versus your peers? What is the earned income per marketing staff? What are marketing expenditures per staff member?

Too many institutions react to financial crises by automatically reducing the size of all staff departments. If fund-raising and marketing staffs are working effectively, it is counterproductive to reduce their size. In fact, it is frequently necessary to *increase* staff size in these departments during fiscal crises. It is hard to find situations where the addition of strong development personnel did not result in substantially more revenue than expense.

Of course, not all staff members are equally strong, and every arts organization must develop a staff evaluation process of some kind. Without a personnel review program, it is difficult to ensure that all staff members are being given appropriate feedback on performance and that a proper paper trail has been established for those personnel members who should be dismissed. The size and complexity of this system will vary; installing a highly structured process can frequently result in "evaluation backlash," with few personnel actively participating in the system.

Ideally, the evaluation process affects salary decisions. Better employees should be rewarded with better salaries. Yet the level of salaries in most arts organization is low, and the budget available for raises so small, that it is difficult to reward the best employees in any meaningful way. One solution is to plan multiyear raises for the best employees. If the funds are not available to give an appropriate raise this year, spread the raise over two or three years, giving the special employees an understanding of their value to the organization and the benefit to them of remaining with the organization.

Finding these special employees is exceedingly difficult, particularly for the most senior positions in an arts organization. Many institutions have turned to executive search firms to fill senior positions; others have created board-managed search committees. In either case, a clear understanding of the needs of the institution, an important element of a carefully constructed plan, is an essential prerequisite to initiating a successful search.

Indeed the focus of all personnel and organizational planning must be on attracting the best arts administrators possible. While one can discuss planning methodologies for days, the truth is that without the right team of implementers, no plan will be effective. And a strong entrepreneurial manager, of whom there are far too few, will outperform a poorly managed institution with a comprehensive plan. The combination of a strong plan and a strong team of managers properly organized is, of course, ideal.

ORGANIZATION PLANNING ISSUES

Each of the following issues should be addressed in the organizational plan for the board:

- Does the structure of the organization support the strategies in the plan?
- Is each department right-sized?
- Are we adequately compensating our best staff?
- How can staff creativity be fostered?
- How can interdepartmental communications be maximized?
- Should the culture of the organization be changed to allow for growth?
- Does the organization have a personnel review policy?
- Are we training our staff?
- Is staff turnover very high? Why? How can this be fixed?

12

*Perhaps the greatest changes to the arts experienced over the
past twenty-five years have resulted from the development of new
technologies. New technologies have changed the way we operate,
the way we sell tickets, the way we engage audiences and donors,
the way we market our work, and even the way we make work. New
technologies have also created new competitors for our audience's
time and attention. It is imperative that every arts organization
plan how it is going to embrace technology so that the organization
remains relevant and accessible to its target audiences and so that
scarce resources can be spent effectively.*

A technology plan should address five basic uses of technology:

Operations. While not necessarily the most newsworthy use, technology allows us to improve the efficiency of most operations of an arts
organization. From managing large databases of audience names or donors to sending out routine notifications to all of our family members
and simplifying the ticketing system, technology has revolutionized the
way we do business in the arts as in other industries. Yet many arts institutions have access to only modest amounts of technical expertise.
Ensuring that organizations have a plan for improving efficiency at an
affordable cost is one important aspect of a technology strategy.

Marketing. Marketing programs have been more affected by technology than any other aspect of our work. Over the past twenty-five years,
websites have become a standard marketing tool of most arts institutions. Over this period, the way we use websites and the way we design
them has changed. It is no longer enough to have a website; the website
must continually change and engage visitors. Arts institutions that have
not evaluated the potency of their websites must plan to do so. Email
blasts are a second major use of technology to improve marketing reach.
Email blasts can include far more information than a direct-mail piece
at a far lower cost. We can include videos, biographies, quotes from critics, and more, since online space is virtually free. For this reason, careful

design of emails is essential, and building the email list is a critical aspect of the plans for many arts institutions.

Of course, social networking is another method for using new technologies to improve marketing effectiveness, while also lowering marketing cost. Planning in this arena must address how the organization will ensure that it is focused on the most popular platforms as they change. Too many organizations are wed to platforms that are not necessarily the ones favored by their target audience groups anymore.

Reaching new audiences. Technology allows arts organizations to reach new audiences, especially those in new geographic areas. Online broadcasts of performances, speeches, and symposia; electronic databases of museum collections; and online education modules all provided access to organizational activities to far more people without respect to geography. Many organizations, for example, have begun to put performances, educational programming, and lectures and symposia online, often via a YouTube channel. These major arts institutions are becoming global forces through their online activities, making it challenging for small and midsized arts organizations to compete. A detailed technology plan will address how the organization plans to make its work available to a broader base of family members and how it will continue to engage this larger family.

Programming. While technology has always affected our performances — from the introduction of stage lighting to the use of electronic sound boards — new technologies are permitting a range of remarkable special effects, expanded use of video, and entirely new modes of art, including virtual reality, augmented reality, and holography. When the Los Angeles Philharmonic mounted its Immortal Beethoven festival, it created a virtual reality experience and allowed Los Angelenos to experience it on a mobile van that drove through the city. Not every organization must embrace new modes of expression, but arts organizations must have plans to learn and consider new technologies, and to invest the resources necessary to do, if the artistic leadership plans to adjust the fundamental nature of the art itself.

Maintaining links to audience members and donors. A newer use of technology is to engage with visitors while they are at the museum or theater and then maintain connections through online activities. Capturing the email addresses of visitors is essential for ensuring that an enduring link can be created. Many arts institutions are creating new ways to engage with visitors to allow for postvisit communications.

Arts organizations must also plan for the ways they will access technological expertise. Only the largest arts organizations can afford to hire in-house technology experts. Many smaller organizations must engage consulting firms to manage IT needs. Joint ventures are a smart way to extend resources for many arts organizations. And creating a technology committee of local technology experts is another way to engage expertise without having to pay for full-time staff.

Questions to be addressed include the following:

- Do we have the technology expertise we need?
- If not, how will we get it?
- Do we have the internal operating systems we need to manage our artistic, marketing, fund-raising, and financial operations?
- What systems should we be adding in the years to come?
- Do we use technology to make our programmatic marketing campaigns more efficient and effective?
- Is our website all it needs to be?
- Do we use social media effectively?
- How many names are on our email list?
- Have we used technology to reach new audiences?
- Are we using new technologies to enhance our art-making?
- Are we good at keeping in touch with audience members and visitors via new technologies?

IMPLEMENTATION PLANNING

The Rubber Meets the Road

13

An implementation plan represents the distillation of the entire strategic planning effort. Many plans lack a clear description of the way each strategy will be put into action. This leaves so many questions unanswered that it is unlikely that many, if any, of the strategies will be pursued. The implementation plan answers three central questions for each strategy:

1. What are the specific steps required to implement the strategy?
2. Who is responsible for implementing the strategy?
3. When will the strategy be implemented?

In a well-designed planning process, one begins to address implementation issues during the strategy development phase.

While creating a realistic implementation plan must be approached with great care, no "surprises" should emerge in the process. Certainly not every strategy can, or should, be implemented immediately. Yet if one or several strategies cannot be implemented at all, owing to a lack of funds, expertise, or time, errors were made in developing the internal analysis or strategies.

There are two central elements in an implementation plan: a list of short-term priorities and a complete discussion of the proposed action steps.

The first task in completing an implementation plan is to identify the key strategies that must be pursued in the very near term. This list will include the most urgent strategies—those that will set the stage for future strategy implementation or will allow the organization to survive. Since many arts organizations approach planning in a serious way only when they are in deep financial trouble, the short-term implementation plan frequently addresses approaches to finding cash immediately. It is important to note that the strategies selected for immediate implementation are not necessarily those that are the most important in the long term. If the organization cannot survive the short term, however, the long-term strategies have little meaning. The entire staff and board must agree to the items on the short-term list, since most will be called upon to implement them. In short, this list represents the organization's work plan for the next six to twelve months.

The second element of the implementation plan is a report that details the steps required to pursue each strategy in the plan as well as the personnel responsible and expected completion date for each step. Each strategy in the short-term priorities list as well as all other strategies mentioned in the plan is included in this report.

Not every strategy can be pursued at the same time. Scarce personnel and financial resources limit the number of strategies that can be addressed at any one time. In addition, some can be pursued only after others have been implemented. For example, a capital campaign will be far more effective after the implementation of a serious institutional marketing effort. An effort to build a high-level individual donor base must also typically follow the strengthening of the board, since board members are invariably central to identifying new donor prospects.

Therefore, it is important to schedule each strategy in relation to the others and with consideration for the total resources available for strategic initiatives. Ideally, implementation plans are developed by the administrative leadership, with assistance from senior staff members, since they tend to have the best idea of the human and financial resources available and the other obligations of the organization.

It is helpful to schedule the major strategies first. For example, the five major strategies for a small opera company are as follows:

- Hiring a new executive director
- Developing high-impact, community-based cultural projects
- Bringing fund-raising activities in-house
- Enhancing marketing and public relations activities
- Involving new board members in fund-raising activities

The first-level implementation plan might include some of the strategies shown in Table 4.

After the basic strategies have been arrayed, the operating steps required for pursuing each strategy can be developed. This list should be detailed enough to provide adequate direction to the implementers. If additional substeps are obvious, they need not be listed. For example, if an organization decides it must hire a new executive director, it might create the action steps shown in Table 5.

Table 4. Implementation Plan

Strategy		FY18	FY19	FY20
A	Hire a new executive director	x		
B	Develop community projects	x	x	
C	Bring fundraising in-house	x		
D	Initiate marketing/PR program	x	x	
E	Engage new board members		Ongoing	

Table 5. Implementation Plan

Strategy	Person responsible	Completion date (FY18 FY19 FY20 FY21 FY22)
A. Hire a new executive director	AD/SC	FY18
Develop job description	SC	FY18—January
Advertise position	MD	FY18—January
Hold preliminary interviews	AD/SC	FY18—January
Hold final interview	AD/SC	FY18—February
Introduce finalist to board/staff	D	FY18—February
Make offer	Board chair	FY18—February

Table 6. Implementation Plan

Strategy	Person responsible	Completion date
B. Initiate marketing/PR program	ED/DD	FY18 and FY19
Communicate leadership in all materials	ED	Ongoing
Create board marketing committee	ED/MD/D	FY18—September
Target "special" individual donors	ED/MD/D	Ongoing
Provide national press with information	ED/MD	Ongoing
Develop design for all print materials	MD/MC	FY18—October
Create in-theater marketing program	ED/MD	FY18—May
Enhance gala benefits	ED/AD/MD/D	Ongoing

Staff		Board	
AD	artistic director	D	directors
ED	executive director	NC	nominating committee
DD	development director	MC	marketing committee
MD	marketing director	SC	search committee

Table 7. Strategy Implementation Chart January–December fiscal year

Strategy	Person responsible	Completion date
A. Hire a new executive director	AD/SC	
Develop job description	SC	FY18—January
Advertise position	MD	FY18—January
Hold preliminary interviews	AD/SC	FY18—January
Hold final interview	AD/SC	FY18—February
Introduce finalist to board/staff	D	FY18—February
Make offer	Board chair	FY18—February
B. Develop community projects	AD/ED	
Define project	AD	FY18—May
Identify facility for project	ED	FY18—July
Schedule activities	ED	FY19—August
Notify participants	AD	FY19—October
Conduct program	AD	FY20—January
C. Bring fundraising in-house	ED	
Hire development associate	AD/ED	FY18—April
Move files to home office	DD	FY18—April
Seek multiyear support for GOS	DD/ED	Ongoing
Establish corporate committee	DD/ED/D	FY19—June
Research support for audience development	D	Ongoing
Seek funds from state/local representatives	ED/DD/D	Ongoing
D. Initiate marketing/PR program	ED/DD	
Communicate leadership in all materials	ED	Ongoing
Create board marketing committee	ED/MD/D	FY18—September
Target "special" individual donors	ED/MD/D	Ongoing
Provide national press with information	ED/MD	Ongoing
Develop design for all print materials	MD/MC	FY18—October
Create in-theater marketing program	ED/MD	FY19—May
Enhance gala benefits	ED/AD/MD/D	Ongoing
E. Engage new board members	ED/AD/D	
Create nominating committee	ED/AD/D	FY18—May
Identify events for cultivating trustees	ED/AD/D/NC	Ongoing
Add contributing board members	ED/NC	Ongoing
Develop board support materials	DD/NC	FY18—June
Annual board retreat	ED/D	Ongoing
Implement orientation process	ED/AD/NC/D	FY18—January
Remove uninvolved board members	ED/NC/D	Ongoing

If another strategy is to develop the organization's marketing/PR program, the implementation steps might include those shown in Table 6.

The final element of the implementation plan is the assignment of responsibility for each operating step. The selection of the implementer will depend upon each candidate's expertise, availability, and interest. An effort must be made to spread the implementation duties among the various staff departments and board committees. If too many implementation steps are assigned to one person, it is unlikely they will be pursued in a timely manner. If one staff member is assigned a disproportionate number of implementation steps, this person is either not a good delegator or the remainder of the staff is not adequate, or both.

Frequently, readers of a detailed plan (including many board members) will fear that the plan is too ambitious, attempting to accomplish too much too soon. A well-crafted implementation plan should allay this concern, although many lay people would be astonished to learn how much each arts professional can accomplish with little support and fewer financial resources. In fact, a great deal must be accomplished, all at the same time. The links between marketing programs and fundraising success, board development and financial health, appropriate staffing and artistic quality, and so forth, are evident. No arts organization has the luxury of waiting for the implementation of any one strategy to be completed before the next is initiated. Arts administrators, like puppeteers, are challenged to handle many actions coincidentally, pulling the appropriate string at the strategic moment.

After the action steps have been developed, they can be scheduled as well. Please note that some strategies that may be fully implemented at a later date (e.g., mounting an additional production) may require some preparatory steps in the near term (e.g., determining the subscribers' interest in an additional production).

FINANCIAL PLANNING AND MANAGEMENT

14

While the missions of not-for-profit arts organizations focus on the delivery of their artistic and educational offerings, it is a fact of life that these organizations must remain in long-term cash flow balance if they are to sustain their levels of performance.

Financial plans are a series of projections that reveal the expected fiscal implications of pursuing the strategies described in the plan. If an organization plans to mount an active national visibility campaign, the associated costs should be reflected in the projected marketing budgets. If strengthening the board to increase contributions from individuals is a key strategy, support from individual donors will grow more rapidly than from other donor categories; fund-raising costs will probably increase as well.

While the financial plan, therefore, is a logical ending point for the strategic planning document, its placement does not mean that the goal of the plan for any arts organization is simply to produce a sound income statement or balance sheet. *The goal of the plan is to help the organization achieve its mission; the financial plan indicates whether the organization will have the fiscal strength to pursue this mission in a consistent manner.*

Two basic structures form the heart of a financial plan: income statements and balance sheets. These reveal the annual fiscal performance of the organization and the accumulated historical level of performance, respectively. The financial plan should project income statements and balance sheets for each year in the planning period.

The number of years in the planning period should depend on the nature of the organization, the challenges it faces, and the stability of the environment. Most organizations project five years into the future when developing their plans. This is sufficient time to implement most strategies and to observe their financial impact. For very young organizations (which change too dramatically to project accurately too far into the future) or for those in a rapidly changing and unstable environment, a three-year forecast may be more reasonable. An organization planning a large-scale physical expansion project, including a capital campaign, however, may need to extend the planning period.

THE INCOME STATEMENT

The income statement for any given year indicates how well the organization performed, on a financial basis, for that year alone. When developed with great care, a projected income statement can become the basis for the budgeting process. Developing these projected income statements requires a careful analysis of anticipated expenses, earned income, and contributed income.

Table 8. Projected Operating Results ($'000)

	Actual	Actual	Est.	Projected	Projected	Projected	Projected	Projected
Unearned income	FY18	FY19	FY20	FY21	FY22	FY23	FY24	FY25
Foundations	$409	$322	$573	$602	$635	$660	$680	$700
Corporations	61	56	70	82	95	105	110	120
Individuals	508	688	844	949	1,045	1,104	1,165	1,228
Federal— operating/challenge	124	340	167	177	47	48	48	49
State/county	20	29	30	32	33	33	34	35
Total unearned income	1,122	1,435	1,684	1,842	1,855	1,950	2,037	2,132
Earned income								
Box office	494	587	719	900	945	983	1,012	1,043
Interest/investments	41	64	124	127	132	137	142	147
Rentals/ads/other	46	149	47	77	87	97	102	113
Total earned income	581	800	890	1,104	1,164	1,217	1,256	1,303
Total income	**$1,703**	**$2,235**	**$2,574**	**$2,946**	**$3,019**	**$3,167**	**$3,293**	**$3,435**
Expenses								
Administrative salaries	$303	$392	$417	$535	$552	$569	$587	$604
Artist/technical salaries	629	945	1,100	1,169	1,199	1,238	1,272	1,317
Employee benefits	76	100	115	112	115	119	122	126
Production/housing	280	484	566	631	661	686	723	761
Educational program	14	13	27	30	33	37	42	48
Administrative expenses	113	151	147	150	155	162	170	180
Marketing/PR	78	99	102	112	123	136	145	155
Fundraising expenses	68	16	17	24	26	28	30	32
General operating	132	138	178	183	187	192	202	212
Total expenses	**$1,693**	**$2,338**	**$2,669**	**$2,946**	**$3,051**	**$3,167**	**$3,293**	**$3,435**
Surplus/(deficit)	10	−103	−95	0	−32	0	0	0

Projecting Unearned Income

It is typically more difficult to forecast levels of contributed income, since a few major gifts won or lost can have a substantial impact on total contributed revenue. A forecast that adds a base of "solid" grants to a reasonable level of unanticipated gifts (depending on the scope of the fund-raising strategies) is the most rational method for projecting unearned income. It is helpful to forecast contributions by category; this increases the chances that errors of optimism and pessimism will cancel each other.

Government Agencies

In general, projections for government funding should remain very conservative, frequently showing no growth at all. If the internal and external analyses suggest that the institution has been negligent in its fund-raising efforts (e.g., failing to apply for government grants for which they are eligible), projections from this source might include increases.

Foundations

Projections for changes in foundation giving will vary depending on the slate of projects contained in the plan and the level of effort devoted to foundation research and relationship development. Substantial educational and other program initiatives are often the most likely to attract new foundation funding. In most regions, the number of relevant foundations is small enough that a forecast for each major foundation can be developed.

Corporations

The rate of funding growth projected from corporate donors will depend on the organization's visibility strategy, the accessibility of the artistic product, the uniqueness of planned programs, and the strength of board relationships with the corporate community. Organizations that plan to strengthen their boards by adding corporate leaders can safely project increases.

Individuals

Unless an active program to increase gifts from individuals is pursued, the total value of these gifts will tend to grow rather slowly. If an organization's board is strengthened and the board members begin to play a more active role in the development effort, or if major institutional marketing campaigns are mounted, gifts from individuals can grow very quickly. The portion of the individual campaign coming from board members should not be difficult to forecast; multiplying the number of board members by the minimum level of board gift, and adding in the extraordinary gifts one anticipates from selected board members, should produce a sensible forecast.

Special Events

Anticipated revenue from special events will also depend on the size and stature of the board, the visibility of the organization, and the nature of the planned events. Multiplying the projected number of tickets sold by the ticket price, adding anticipated underwriting, and subtracting budgeted expenses yields a solid forecast of net income.

Capital Campaigns

Capital campaigns are almost always multiyear projects. Therefore, an extended budgeting format must be employed to ensure that cash will be available to cover all programmatic and campaign costs.

A practical, long-range projection for a capital campaign should include a revenue projection and an expenditure schedule. The projections for a capital campaign will depend largely on the results of a feasibility study. A carefully crafted feasibility study should indicate the timing and level of net campaign revenue (campaign revenue minus the costs of administering the campaign).

The capital campaign analysis must reveal accumulated cash on hand (or a shortfall of cash). This will help determine when and for how long a temporary excess of cash should be invested and when shortfalls will necessitate a bridge loan to complete the project.

Projecting Earned Income

Touring. Revenues from tour fees cannot be projected without considering the associated expenses. Many organizations lose money on tour, since the direct touring expenses exceed fees. For these organizations, an increase in touring activity *reduces* net income unless the larger tour is a more rational one—reducing per-performance costs by

Table 9. Capital Campaign Schedule $5.0 million goal ($'000)

I. Gifts and grants	FY18	FY19	FY20	FY21	FY22
A. Pledge schedule	$2,500	$1,500	$750	$250	0
B. Pledge receipts	800	2,200	1,000	700	300

II. Use of pledge receipts					
A. Reduce cumulative deficit	200	100	0	0	0
B. Cash reserve	0	550	200	0	0
C. New/upgraded facility					
1. Purchase	250	1,450	0	0	0
2. Construction	0	0	750	700	300
3. Feeds (preclosing and closing)	250	0	0	0	0
D. Campaign expenses (5% of total)	100	80	50	20	0
Total use of campaign pledges	**800**	**2,180**	**1,000**	**720**	**300**
Remaining campaign funds— cumulative	$0	$20	$20	$0	$0
Interest revenue (7%)	0	0	1	0	0

increasing efficiency. Other organizations simply break even on tour. For these organizations, the projected level of touring does not affect net financial performance (apart from its impact on meeting union requirements for weeks of employment for the artists). In this situation, the level of touring does have an impact on visibility—regional, national, or international. Exploited appropriately, this visibility should translate into opportunities to increase fundraising revenues.

Ticket sales or admissions. Growth in admissions and ticket sales is not simply a matter of luck, inflation, or operating in a larger facility. Attendance increases when programming and marketing efforts justify larger attendance. The artistic and marketing plans should have an explicit impact on the forecast levels of earned revenue.

To determine the growth rate of earned income, one must evaluate current attendance levels, the capacity of the facility, the number of performances or exhibitions, the nature of the proposed repertory, the effectiveness of the current marketing effort and plans for changes in the effort, proposed changes in the cost of admission, and the expected activities of peer companies competing for the same audience. Each of these factors will have a substantial impact on projected earned-income levels; the challenge is to estimate the effect of each factor in a reasonable manner. Overly optimistic forecasts can place the future of the organization in jeopardy and certainly reduce the credibility of the entire plan. Overly conservative forecasts hamper the organization's ability to achieve its mission.

Interest income. Projected changes in endowment levels and working capital reserve funds will affect projections for interest revenue. An appropriate interest rate forecast can be obtained from the organization's bank or from a board member who works in the financial community.

Table 10. Earned Income Worksheet

Theater One	Actual FY18	Estimate FY19	Projected FY20	Projected FY21	Projected FY22	Projected FY23	Projected FY24
Number of performances	140	140	140	140	140	154	154
Number of seats	1,200	1,200	1,200	1,200	1,200	1,200	1,200
Total seating capacity	168,000	168,000	168,000	168,000	168,000	184,800	184,800
Percentage of capacity sold	65%	65%	60%	64%	70%	70%	75%
Total seats sold	109,200	109,200	100,800	107,520	117,600	129,360	138,600
Average ticket price	20.00	21.00	21.00	21.50	22.00	23.00	23.00
Ticket sales/Theater One	2.18M	2.29M	2.12M	2.31M	2.59M	2.98M	3.19M
Change from previous year	8%	5%	−8%	9%	12%	15%	7%
Theater Two							
Number of performances	0	0	60	70	80	80	90
Number of seats	0	0	200	200	200	200	200
Total seating capacity	0	0	12,000	14,000	16,000	16,000	18,000
Percentage of capacity sold	0%	0%	50%	55%	60%	65%	70%
Total seats sold	0	0	6,000	7,700	9,600	10,400	12,600
Average ticket price	0.00	0.00	9.50	10.00	10.50	11.00	11.50
Ticket sales/Theater Two	0	0	57,000	77,000	100,800	114,400	144,900
Change from previous year	N/A	N/A	N/A	35%	31%	13%	27%
Rental income (Theater Two)							
Weeks available to rent	0	0	12	11	10	10	10
Weekly rental fees	0	0	10,000	10,500	11,000	11,500	12,000
Rental income	0	0	120,000	115,500	110,000	115,000	120,000
Change from previous year	N/A	N/A	N/A	−4%	−5%	5%	4%
Total	2.18M	2.29M	2.29M	2.50M	2.80M	3.21M	3.45M
Change from previous year	8%	5%	0%	9%	12%	15%	8%

Table 11. Endowment from Capital Campaign $7.0 million goal ($'000)

I. Campaign endowment	Current FY18	Budget FY19	Projected FY20	Projected FY21	Projected FY22	Projected FY23
A. Endowment principal year start	$2,366	$2,366	$4,891	$6,959	$8,118	$9,391
B. Additions from campaign	0	2,500	2,000	1,000	1,000	500
Total endowment principal	2,366	4,866	6,891	7,959	9,118	9,891
C. Projected income	118	268	413	557	729	692
Endowment principal plus income	2,484	5,134	7,304	8,516	9,847	10,583
D. Less: income for operations (5%)	——	——	——	——	——	——
	(118)	(243)	(345)	(398)	(456)	(495)
Endowment principal at year end	$2,366	$4,891	$6,959	$8,118	$9,391	$10,088
Percentage change from previous year	N/A	107%	42%	17%	16%	7%

The growth in the endowment and working capital reserve funds will depend on any plans for a capital campaign, projected annual operating surpluses (or deficits), and the use of income from these funds. Most organizations take as operating income only a set percent of the endowment fund each year, leaving any additional income in the fund to accommodate inflation. It is not uncommon to "take" 5 percent of the balance of the endowment fund at the start of the fiscal year as operating income, leaving the remaining realized income in the fund. (Some organizations use a three-year average of the starting endowment balance to calculate this income level to protect against sudden changes in the value of the endowment portfolio.)

Interest earned by the reserve fund should remain in that fund to compensate for inflation and for anticipated budget growth. This helps to maintain the reserve's effectiveness in the future.

Other earned income. The income earned on merchandise sales, food concessions, souvenir books, and so on, is usually tied directly to attendance. The analysis underlying the forecasts of ticket sales and attendance fees should be used to generate other earned-income projections.

Projecting Expenses

Projecting expense growth (or reduction) in each budget category for each year of the planning period is a time-consuming activity. It is helpful to create a work sheet that shows the projected timing and cost

Table 12. Expense Projections ($'000)

Marketing expenses personnel	Estimate FY18	Projected FY19	Projected FY20	Projected FY21	Projected FY22	Projected FY23
Base staff salaries	$415	$415	$457	$475	$509	$530
New marketing associate	0	25	0	15	0	0
Employee benefits (20%)	83	88	91	98	102	106
Total personnel costs	**$498**	**$528**	**$548**	**$588**	**$611**	**$636**
Marketing/PR						
Ongoing programs	$100	$104	$108	$112	$117	$122
Create new press materials	0	10	0	0	0	7
Expand direct mail	0	7	10	10	12	15
Hire press agent	0	0	10	15	18	20
Total marketing/PR costs	$100	$121	$128	$137	$147	$164
Total marketing expenses	**$598**	**$649**	**$676**	**$725**	**$758**	**$800**
Change from previous year	N/A	8.5%	4.2%	7.2%	4.5%	5.5%

Average annual increase in marketing: 6.7%

of each strategic initiative. These costs are added to the base-year budget (plus any expected inflation) to show the projected expense levels.

All anticipated changes in an organization's operations, whether or not they are a direct result of the planning process, must be reflected in these expense projections. This requires a good deal of thought. For example, if a new staff position is added to create an institutional marketing program, the estimated added salary expense should obviously be included in the appropriate budget category. Yet the addition of this position will also create ancillary costs raising printing, telephone, materials, and other associated budgets.

This means that the requirements for implementing each strategy must be carefully considered. The implementation chart described in the previous chapter is a useful tool for guiding this analysis.

THE BALANCE SHEET

Arts organizations frequently focus on only the income statement. In fact, most plans tend to omit balance sheet forecasts entirely, ignoring the impact of balance sheet accounts on the institution's long-term fiscal health. While income statement projections depict an organization's anticipated annual activity on a year-to-year basis, balance sheet projections forecast its progress establishing financial stability. The process of developing balance sheet forecasts is very straightforward if income statement and capital campaign forecasts have been completed. For apart from these variables, balance sheet items tend to move in very predictable (or offsetting) ways: long-term debt is paid off according to schedule, depreciation is similarly scheduled, and so forth.

Table 13. Pro Forma Balance Sheet: Operating Fund Projections ($'000)

Assets	Actual	Actual	Estimated	Projected	Projected	Projected	Projected	Projected
Current assets	FY18	FY19	FY20	FY21	FY22	FY23	FY24	FY25
Cash	$48	$69	$25	$80	$140	$114	$118	$112
Loans receivable	3	3	3	13	13	13	13	13
Accounts/pledges receivable	325	289	287	285	275	270	275	275
Grants receivable	300	155	155	155	155	170	170	185
Prepaid expenses	54	48	48	48	48	48	54	60
Total current assets	730	564	518	581	631	615	630	645
Noncurrent assets								
Loans receivable	9	6	6	6	6	6	6	6
Pledges receivable	458	230	230	230	230	220	240	255
Grants receivable	250	130	130	130	130	130	130	130
Due from other	87	75	75	50	0	0	0	0
Total noncurrent assets	804	441	441	416	366	356	376	391
Total assets	$1,534	$1,005	$959	$997	$997	$971	$1,006	$1,036

Liabilities	Actual	Actual	Estimated	Projected	Projected	Projected	Projected	Projected
Current liabilities	FY18	FY19	FY20	FY21	FY22	FY23	FY24	FY25
Note payable	$180	$81	$106	$40	$20	$0	$0	$0
Accounts payable	48	45	90	26	46	40	40	40
Deferred revenue	590	584	564	564	564	564	564	564
Total current assets	818	710	760	630	630	604	604	604
Long-term liabilities								
Long-term debt	10	7	7	7	7	7	7	7
Deferred revenues	696	360	360	360	360	360	395	425
Long-term debt	706	367	367	367	367	367	402	432
Total	$1,524	$1,077	$1,127	$997	$997	$971	$1,006	$1,036
Fund balance	10	(72)	(168)	0	0	0	0	0
Total liabilities and fund balance	$1,534	$1,005	$959	$997	$997	$971	$1,006	$1,036

FINANCIAL ANALYSIS

For many readers of the plan, the income statement and balance sheet forecasts will not be meaningful. It is incumbent on the planner to produce measures and analyses derived from these forecasts that communicate their implications. Some clearly understood measures include the following.

Operating Fund Balance

Eliminating operating deficits is frequently an organizational priority. An operating surplus is an indication that an organization has taken responsibility for supporting its programs. It is also a sign to vendors, funders, banks, and potential board members that the organization's staff and board assume a businesslike approach to resource management.

Net Current Assets Position

Net current assets, calculated by subtracting current liabilities from current assets, is a basic indicator of the institution's ability to fund day-to-day operating requirements. Positive net current assets indicates that the organization has more short-term assets than short-term debts; meeting current obligations should not be a problem. Many organizations have negative net current assets, indicating that they do not have the resources to cover short-term commitments. In other words, these organizations are facing a cash flow crisis.

Working Capital Reserve Fund

Soon after achieving a balanced operating fund, the institution should consider establishing a working capital reserve fund that provides short-term loans to the institution as cash flow needs dictate. The organization must repay this internal loan by the end of the fiscal year to maintain the viability of this internal line of credit.

Endowment Fund

Endowments are particularly important to institutions that are limited in their ability to develop sufficient levels of earned or unearned income. For example, most museums cannot achieve substantial levels of earned income. This has encouraged museums to build large endowment funds. The advisability of creating an operating endowment for a performing arts organization is questionable. The amount of money that must be raised compared to the annual income resulting from the fund discourages many organizations from pursuing endowments actively. (Those organizations with an aging base of donors must consider the establishment of an endowment, possibly through planned giving.)

The way these financial measures are displayed will vary depending on the tastes of the board and financial staff. The financial projections included in the strategic plan should be scrutinized by the planning committee, the executive committee, the development committee, the finance committee, and the marketing committee before being presented to the board for final approval.

FINANCIAL MANAGEMENT

Just as strategies are effective only if they are well implemented, financial forecasts are relevant only if the fiscal management of the organization is strong. The plan must address deficiencies in the budgeting and control mechanisms in addition to including the forecasts described above. While a financial system must be custom-made to suit the specific needs of the organization, all such systems share certain processes, including budget preparation, performance monitoring, cash flow analysis, and control.

Many arts institutions do not begin their annual budgeting processes early enough to affect many decisions that have a substantial financial impact. Too often, selection of repertory, for example, precedes budget development, reducing the ability of the budget process to affect the majority of expense decisions.

Financial performance must be closely monitored to allow for mid-season changes in course. Monthly reporting is necessary. Senior staff members and the board's finance committee should receive appropriate summary and detail reports and a narrative that describes unanticipated changes in revenue and expense projections. These monthly reports should also describe the difference between actual performance and the budgeted level. The narrative must explain why major variances occurred and their impact on projected year-end results. Organizations that experience wide swings in cash flow will need to budget on a monthly basis. Those that enjoy more even cash flows can avoid monthly budgets and can compare actual year-to-date results to a corresponding proportion of the annual budget.

Cash flow projections are a critical management tool, revealing when financial stress will be at its high and low ebb. For stable institutions, those with large cash reserves, monthly cash flow projections are usually adequate. They suggest when excess cash might be available for investment. Organizations facing cash crises must work week by week. Discussions on payment deferrals with vendors, unions, and banks must be supported by accurate cash flow projections.

In the short term, the budget is the most important financial management tool, since it is a direct expression of an organization's operational objectives. The budgeting process will often encourage healthy discussions regarding organizational priorities. Managing the annual budget process is usually the responsibility of the top administrative and financial staff.

The projected changes in year-end financial results should have an impact on current activities. If an organization expects to fall far short of revenue projections, earned or contributed, either expenditures must be cut or additional revenue-generating programs must be implemented. Too many organizations simply report on the financial results without taking remedial action to address shortfalls.

Those organizations with strong fiscal management systems, with boards that feel well informed (and warned of impending crises), and with the ability to project financial performance with some degree of accuracy earn the respect of the entire community. This respect is an important asset, helping the organization attract new board members, additional contributors, larger contributions from current donors, and the assistance of vendors, donors, the board, and the staff during periods of crisis and in support of special campaigns. In short, those organizations that display a high level of fiscal responsibility are also the ones that will have the resources they need to achieve their missions well into the future.

The financial plan, therefore, must address how and when the organization is going to create a healthier financial management system.

PART 4 Planning for Planning

A PLAN FOR PLANNING
The Planning Process

15

While it is essential to ensure that an arts organization's strategic plan has insightful, rich content, many planning efforts fail because the planning processes they employ are poorly designed. If important participants are left out of planning activities, if the planning process moves at a snail's pace, or if insufficient (or extravagant) resources are employed, an organization can easily begin to suffer from planning backlash, finding it is difficult to get *anyone* interested in creating, implementing, or even discussing the plan.

The previous chapters of this book focused on planning content; this chapter reviews a suggested planning process. In other words, while the focus to this point has been on developing effective plans, we now turn to the important issue of doing this in an efficient manner. A four-phase, eleven-step process is recommended:

Phase I. Setting Up
Step 1. Committing resources
Step 2. Adopting a framework
Step 3. Establishing a planning calendar
Step 4. Writing a mission statement

Phase II. Analyzing
Step 5. Collecting data
Step 6. Performing external and internal analyses

Phase III. Strategizing
Step 7. Developing strategies
Step 8. Creating an implementation plan
Step 9. Completing financial forecasts

Phase IV. Implementing
Step 10. Communicating the plan
Step 11. Tracking and revising

PHASE I. SETTING UP

Given the time and money needed to develop a comprehensive plan, it is essential to begin by creating a plan for planning. The discussions on participants, resources, calendars, and so forth, that preface the planning process set the stage for the entire process.

Step 1. Committing Resources

Although the decision to develop a strategic plan is often made without a great deal of forethought (but with the sense that planning is "good for you"), every organization must think carefully about the time and financial resources it is willing to commit.

While plans can be developed in many different ways, significant staff and board time is required in any effective planning process. Ideally, one member of the board or the staff will have substantial planning experience, and the time required, to guide the process as the planning coordinator. While a good plan will represent a consensus of staff and board views, a strong leader is needed to ensure consistent progress toward developing that consensus. If no one on the staff or the board has the time or expertise required to lead the planning process, an outside consultant should be engaged. One caution about hiring consultants: while an experienced, sensitive consultant can be an invaluable aid, the staff and the board are responsible for implementing the plan, not the consultant. Therefore, while the consultant can be useful in guiding the process, collecting and analyzing data, helping to frame strategies, and giving objective reaction to others' ideas, the resulting plan must not be considered the "consultant's strategy." If the organization feels no ownership of the plan, it will not get implemented. (A planning consultant need not be expensive. Board members will often be affiliated with corporations boasting large planning staffs. Frequently a corporate planner will be willing and able to provide pro bono assistance. But this planner must be sensitive to the differences between for-profit and not-for-profit organizations, especially with respect to mission, marketing, and fundraising.) Apart from the hiring of a consultant, the out-of-pocket costs of developing a strategic plan should be minimal.

Ideally, all staff department heads will be involved in the creation of the plan. Of course, the artistic and administrative leaders must also be actively involved. Participating in data collection, analysis, strategy sessions, and review sessions can easily consume two working days per person. A similar amount of time should be committed by the subset of board members who will be responsible for overseeing the development of the plan.

If the board has an executive committee, this is the ideal group to participate in the planning process, although some boards will name a planning committee to serve this function. In either case, it is imperative that the board members who participate in the planning process be the most respected and involved board members, including the board's officers. Plans developed solely by subordinates rarely, if ever, get the appropriate level of board buy-in.

The decision to engage in a planning process should be made only after every participant has agreed to devote the time necessary to create a strong, implementable plan. Without these commitments, and a suitable planning coordinator, the resulting process will usually take too long and result in an unsatisfactory plan.

Step 2. Adopting a Framework

This book has suggested one approach to planning that has been effective in many arts organizations, both large and small. This framework is simply a road map that guides the planning activity. It suggests the analyses that should be performed, reveals the implications of these analyses, and describes how these implications can be used to develop effective strategies. While the framework described in this volume is not the only useful one, some structure must be employed to develop an effective plan in an efficient manner. (Ideally, the framework selected will be familiar to the person serving as planning coordinator.) While brilliant plans have been developed without the use of a framework, rarely, if ever, are these plans developed in an efficient or complete manner. The goal of the framework is to ensure that the plan is developed quickly, with a minimum of frustration and a good deal of rigor.

For the framework to be used effectively, it must be explained to all planning participants. A preliminary planning meeting that reviews the framework should mark the formal start of the planning process.

Step 3. Establishing a Planning Calendar

While the framework details the conceptual flow of information and planning activities, the planning calendar describes the timing, desired output, and accountable participants for each step. Apart from its importance as an organizational tool, the calendar serves as a contract, binding all participants to one work plan and schedule.

The specific calendar will differ by organization, depending on the participants, the framework, the availability of data, the depth of analysis, and the experience of the coordinator. However, as a rule of thumb, a good plan can typically be developed in a four- to six-month time period. If the framework presented in this book is employed, a planning calendar might resemble the one shown here.

In short, each of the steps discussed in this book must be included in the planning calendar. While sufficient time for each analysis must be allocated, the process should not be stretched over an extended period

Table 14. Planning Calendar

Planning step	Elapsed time	Participants
1. Solicit/educate participants	2 weeks	All participants
2. Meeting 1: organizational		
3. Write/review mission	2 weeks	All participants
4. Meeting 2: mission review		
5. Collect data	3 weeks	Coordinator
6. Complete environmental analysis	2 weeks	Coordinator
7. Review environmental analysis	1 week	All participants
8. Perform internal analysis	2 weeks	Coordinator
9. Review internal analysis	1 week	All participants
10. Meeting 3: environmental/internal review		
11. Develop proposed strategies	3 weeks	Coordinator
12. Review and revise strategies	2 weeks	All participants
13. Meeting 4: strategy development		
14. Create implementation plan	1 week	Coordinator
15. Create financial plan	1 week	Coordinator
16. Write draft of plan	1 week	Coordinator
17. Review and revise plan	2 weeks	All participants
18. Meeting 5: Final strategy review		
19. Approval by board		
20. Communicate plan	Ongoing	All participants

of time. Long, drawn-out planning processes tend to result in an unfocused effort, with participants forgetting the conclusions of past meetings and analyses.

It is particularly important that participants remain with the process from beginning to end. While some may "drop out" as the process progresses, it is disadvantageous to add people once planning has commenced. New participants who have not been through the initial stages will force the entire group to retrace its steps, resulting in a loss of momentum.

While there is value in developing plans rapidly, rushing the process can be harmful as well. A good plan involves analysis, creativity, and thought. These cannot be rushed. And achieving consensus is essential for successful implementation; it is important that enough time is allowed for the entire planning group to feel ownership of the document. If the planning coordinator "forces" a plan on the participants, it is unlikely to be implemented successfully.

Step 4. Writing a Mission Statement

The mission statement guides the entire planning process; without it, there is no motivation for planning. While great care must be taken to ensure that the mission statement truly captures the purpose of the organization, it is equally important that writing the statement does not paralyze the planning effort.

Many organizations suffer so much over the drafting of the mission that when it is finally completed, there is little energy left for the remainder of the planning process. While the arguments over the substance of the mission are vital to resolve, the specific choice of words should not become the focus of lengthy discussions. The mission is not an advertising slogan that must be catchy, nor is it poetry that must be inspiring; it is a guiding statement whose *meaning* must be clear.

Each meeting of the planning committee should be motivated by a completed analysis that can provide the basis for discussion. Thoughtful preparation will eliminate many hours of unnecessary discussions. The formulation of the mission is no exception. The planning coordinator, or another member of the planning committee, should draft a proposed mission (or several alternatives) to be distributed prior to the first meeting. While it is unlikely that this statement will remain unchanged, it provides a starting point for discussion. Once the group has agreed on the substance of the mission, a committee member should draft the working mission statement and distribute it to all planning participants. (The arguments over specific wording can then be negotiated between the coordinator and the other participants outside of formal meetings.) If substantive disagreements over the mission persist, a subcommittee of the group including the head of the board and the artistic and administrative leadership of the staff should convene to develop the working mission statement. (Some organizations want the entire board to be involved in drafting the mission statement; this can be rather cumbersome in organizations with sizeable boards.)

It is essential that meetings on the mission statement involve both staff and board members. While it is sometimes efficient to hold separate meetings when reviewing other portions of the plan (e.g., environmental analysis), it is potentially dangerous to hold separate staff discussions on the mission statement. If either the staff or the board become wed to a mission that is not supported by the other group, serious board/staff conflict is inevitable, with the staff leadership placed firmly in the middle.

In some instances the mission statement is not formally adopted until the planning process is completed. Frequently, the environmental and internal analyses will influence the specific elements. The working mission does not become final, therefore, until the planning participants are satisfied that it is appropriate and that the proposed strategic direction is consistent with the mission.

PHASE II: ANALYZING

The best plans are based on thoughtful analysis of key strategic issues; the best planning processes employ analytical tools that reveal these strategic issues in a most efficient manner.

Step 5. Collecting Data

The development of rigorous external and internal analyses rests, in large measure, on the availability of good information. Frequently, organizations spend too little time on data collection because they believe, mistakenly, that all important information is already known. This is a dangerous assumption. Basing a plan on conventional wisdom rather than facts can lead to unrealistic, ineffective strategies.

In truth, collecting the data required for planning in the arts is easy compared to the same task in the for-profit sector. The lack of severe competition, the desire for publicity, the need to provide information to potential donors, and the presence of industry organizations leads arts organizations to publish substantial amounts of information. Most important, the collegial spirit among arts organizations makes the data collection process much more open.

The data upon which planning analyses are based are described in previous chapters. The primary sources for these data include the following:

- Online Searches: A good base of knowledge can be obtained from published articles in newspapers, magazines, and trade journals. DataArts, formerly the Cultural Data Project, collects substantial amounts of data for thousands of arts organizations.
- Industry Associations: There are major industry associations for virtually every art form. Opera America, Dance USA, Association of Art Museum Directors, and the like, all collect information that is available to its members. These data frequently include income statement and balance sheet items for industry participants as well as overall industry trends in major expense and income accounts. This information can provide the basis for industry and peer company analyses. The staffs of these associations frequently possess a great deal of knowledge and insight into their art forms. It is very useful to mine this source of information. Given their desire to be supportive, the industry associations may be willing to review and comment upon an environmental analysis.
- Peer Company Data: Almost every arts organization has a website that will provide important information. Form 990 tax filings are also available on line. But it is critical to note that 990s combine operating and capital revenue and expenses so that organizations can look far larger than they really are if they are in the midst of a capital campaign. If possible, obtain an annual report or audit from a peer company; this will virtually always separate capital and operating accounts.
- Interviews: There are many people knowledgeable about each art form, peer companies, and one's own organization who can pro-

vide useful information for planning analyses. Staff members in peer companies, government agencies, and industry associations can all provide useful information. Of course, all staff heads and involved board members from one's own organization should be asked to provide input to the internal and environmental analyses.

Before these interviews are conducted, however, it is useful to have gathered data from all other sources and have already performed some preliminary analysis. Field interviews are time consuming and should be performed only as needed. It is difficult to know what additional information is needed until substantial data collection and analysis have been performed.

The quality of each analysis depends, in great measure, on the quality of the underlying data. Organizations that spend little time on data collection will have a difficult time developing an objective understanding of the environment in which they operate and of their own strengths and weaknesses. Without this analytical underpinning, it is difficult to write plans that create change.

If the planning coordinator does not have the skill or time to gather the required information, a planning consultant may be employed effectively.

Step 6. Performing External and Internal Analyses

There is a wealth of data that can and should be used to develop a plan; the challenge is to draw insights from these data through environmental and internal analyses. A substantial portion of this book has been devoted to describing the analyses that underlie the development of a strategic plan. While these analyses need not be difficult to perform, the amount of time devoted to them depends on the planners' experience and the desired level of depth.

The application of environmental analysis techniques is perhaps the most challenging part of planning. With some training, however, most people can begin to apply these tools effectively. Yet the challenges are to generate insight from the analysis and to integrate these individual insights into a coherent analysis, or "story line." Without a cohesive story line, it is difficult to communicate results in a manner that allows the eventual plan readers to remember the key issues. Writing a memorable plan is important. Since implementers will need to shift direction as they observe changes in the environment, it is important that they remember the basis upon which the strategies were developed. Few arts administrators have time to refer back to a written document with any frequency. Developing a story line that makes the analysis more memorable is an invaluable implementation tool.

The development of the story line should begin with the commencement of the external analysis. It should not wait until the day before the analysis is due and after all the relevant data have been collected. Just as Sherlock Holmes always had an hypothesis concerning the identity of the criminal, so should the planner always have a theory concerning the driving forces in the industry and the expected behavior of the peer companies. As the hypothesis is disproved by the analysis, it should be reformulated to accommodate the new data.

Before completing any environmental analysis, therefore, it is useful for the planning coordinator to speculate about the results; if the results support the hypothesis, one can proceed to the next step. If, however, the results are not as expected, it means that either the hypothesis is wrong or the analysis was performed incorrectly. Frequently the biggest insights in the analysis process are generated when the expected results and actual results differ.

The planning coordinator must be willing to be cavalier when performing the environmental analysis. It is unlikely that every single piece of desired information will be available, nor will every analysis be completed with a great deal of certainty. Just as in all phases of a creative process, the trade-off between time and product is important; if the analyses are reasonable and insightful, one must be willing to "let go" and move on to the next step of the process even if the underlying data are not as specific as one might have wished. (Frequently, the desired information will emerge later in the planning process anyway.)

The internal analysis must be more specific than the environmental analysis. This is facilitated by a substantially easier data collection job. The difficulty in internal analysis is not so much finding accurate data as it is maintaining honesty and objectivity. As noted in chapter 4, many organizations tend to be overly generous with praise for their own capabilities, while others tend to be too self-critical. A clear, mature evaluation is required. In order to achieve this desired objectivity, the internal analysis should be performed by either a new staff or board member or an outside consultant—someone with planning experience and knowledge of the field but with few historical ties to the organization.

As with environmental analysis, hypotheses about the strengths, weaknesses, culture, and so on, of the organization should be formed as the analysis progresses. Reviewing these hypotheses with staff and board members allows the planning coordinator to test their validity. One-on-one interviews are very important; internal analyses based solely on printed financial data will frequently fail to reveal the motivating factors that can frequently be the most important revelations. If a theater company is managed by an artistic director whose real motivation is to have an opportunity to direct or to act in his own productions, this will have a substantial impact on the functioning of the organization. This information would not emerge from financial or other printed data.

For this reason, internal analysis is not necessarily an enjoyable endeavor. The analysts must question the performance of their own organization. This requires courage, strength, and the open support of the board and the staff. Defensiveness always leads to poor planning.

It is impossible to overemphasize the importance of insightful environmental and internal analyses. The difference between a good strategy and a bad one is frequently the level of understanding that underlies its creation. The development of high-quality analyses will increase the chances of developing a realistic, implementable plan rather than simply a good-looking document.

PHASE III: STRATEGIZING

While a substantial analytical foundation for planning is crucial, the "meat" of the process is the creation of the strategies themselves.

Step 7. Developing Strategies

Just as there is no simple prescription for writing a symphony, so there is no magic formula for creating an effective strategy. Using the framework described in the preceding chapters simply guides the creative thinker.

The most effective way to create a set of integrated strategies is for the planning coordinator to develop a set of proposed strategies, a "straw man plan," upon which the remainder of the group can comment. This yields much better results than placing the entire committee in a room and asking the members to create a plan. Groups tend to go around and around with all members repeating their favorite strategies until they are sure they will be included. These group strategies, typically dominated by the views of the loudest participant, have no focus or, often, much real substance.

Equally dangerous is dividing the strategy development task among separate functional teams (e.g., marketing, development, etc.). While this is an appropriate technique for evaluating strategies or even developing implementation plans, it is not appropriate for developing the strategies of the organization. Every individual strategy must link to and support one overall direction. In fact, one should be able to summarize the key strategies in no more than one page. While many pages of detail might follow this summary, the core of the strategic plan should be an integrated set of actions designed to achieve the mission.

For this reason, having different subcommittees list their strategies for an assigned functional area often results in disjointed, unimplementable plans. Organizations that pursue the "straw man" method of planning find that strategies can be suggested, evaluated in the context of a coherent direction, and adopted or rejected as appropriate.

Step 8. Creating an Implementation Plan

Once agreement on each functional strategy has been reached, the planning committee must develop a detailed implementation plan that suggests how these strategies will be put into action.

If the strategies have been developed in a rigorous manner, the implementation plan should be rather easy to complete. The planning coordinator, with great help from senior staff, should be assigned the task of creating a proposed implementation plan. Since the central issues to be addressed in the implementation plan involve assigning specific tasks and deadlines to key personnel, staff leaders are essential when developing this first draft. They are in a position to know how much can truly be accomplished within realistic time frames.

The board members who serve on the planning committee can then decide whether the proposed implementation plan moves at a realistic pace and is comprehensive enough to be believable.

Step 9. Completing Financial Forecasts

The final section of the plan, the long-term financial forecast, must be developed with great care and realism. For many readers, the forecast will be an indicator of the rigor of the overall plan. If the forecasts are unrealistic or sloppy, the entire planning effort will be undermined.

This does not mean that financial plans should be ultraconservative or should show little change in the fiscal status of the organization. If major new strategic initiatives will be implemented, financial condition is bound to change. But the forecasts must be supported by clear explanations of the reasons for these changes.

Too often, the planning committee is exhausted by the time it comes to develop these forecasts and leaves the job to the staff financial officer. While this is an efficient way to begin, the board representatives must review these forecasts with as much rigor as they review the annual budget. If the plan is taken seriously by the staff and the board, these forecasts will provide the foundation for developing each annual budget during the planning period.

PHASE IV. IMPLEMENTING

The true payoff from planning comes from implementation. Everything accomplished to this point in the planning process is just prologue.

Step 10. Communicating the Plan

The strategic plan should be of interest to many stakeholders: board members, the staff, major contributors, major suppliers, and the press. It is beneficial, therefore, to devote time to developing an appropriate method of communicating the plan with each of these interested parties.

Obviously a complete written document is vital; it provides an easy, convenient reference for everyone. But there are no awards given for length. The "planning by the pound" mentality, which suggests that the heavier the document, the better the plan, misses the point. If implementation is the true end product of planning, then the document must be easy to read and of reasonable length. Rarely should a plan have to exceed seventy-five pages unless an organization is unusually complex.

The "bigger is better" approach is symptomatic of a common misunderstanding about the role of the written document. It is imperative that all planning participants understand that *the planning document is not the plan.* The plan is the common understanding that all strategy implementers have about the direction of the organization. The document itself is not sacred; as time goes on, the plan must be adapted to the changing world.

The simplest way to organize the planning document is to use the framework that underlies the strategy development process. (One hint: the titles for the chapters of this book can easily serve as chapter, or subchapter, headings for the plan.)

When the planning committee has completed its work, the entire board should be asked to read and approve the document. Frequently, some changes to the plan will be requested by those board members who did not serve on the planning committee. Rarely is a carefully crafted plan rejected by the board.

Staff members should also be given an opportunity to read and comment on the plan. Frequently, the staff members who did not serve on the planning committee will have ideas that can strengthen the document.

While many donors, particularly professionally managed foundations, corporations, and government agencies, may have an interest in reviewing the entire document, other donors should be provided with a summarized version that includes the mission, key implications of the environmental and internal analyses, the major strategies, and summary financial projections.

In some organizations, the staff is asked to provide an abbreviated executive summary for the board and donor group. This can prove to be counterproductive. If a reader is not given a sense of the depth of the underlying analysis and thought, the proposed strategies may appear superficial, at best. One must accept that many readers will begin with a prejudice about planning, having taken part in unfocused, unproductive planning efforts. If a synopsis appears superficial, the plan will be deemed superficial.

In-person presentations to groups of donors can be a good way to "engage" them in the functioning of the organization and has the corollary effect of demonstrating professionalism.

Step 11. Tracking and Revising

Since so much time and effort can be devoted to developing a strategic plan, there is a tendency for participants to memorialize their efforts by creating an impressive, leather-bound, formal document. The strategic plan, however, should be a living entity, residing more in the mind than in the bookshelf. The ability to alter the plan as the organization's situation changes is more important than the quality of the binding.

An organization's strategies should not be static. Despite our best efforts to forecast environmental changes, exogenous shocks to the arts environment (e.g., new technologies or radical shifts in government funding) create the need for reevaluation of the strategy. Data collection and analysis leading to periodic reviews must be ongoing.

This tracking process should review industry and peer company behavior, progress toward fulfilling the implementation plan, and financial and other performance measures versus objectives. Tracking the progress of the plan should be performed at regular intervals. Quarterly evaluations are usually sufficient, although in some specific instances (e.g., when large projects are in progress), more frequent ones may be necessary. As deviations from expected results are encountered, strategy alternatives must be developed and implemented.

The results of the tracking process should be presented at board meetings, executive and planning committee meetings, and staff meetings. Once a year, a revised financial plan should be produced. Every three years, a complete new plan should be created. While the mission should not change, and even some strategies may remain consistent, changes to the environment and financial performance are inevitable and the implementation steps must be revised to accommodate changes in staff, board leadership, and so forth.

While the nature of a book forces a presentation of planning activities in a sequential fashion, the steps to creating a superior plan are not necessarily performed in a strictly linear order. Above all, strategizing is a creative process. Blindly following a series of steps impairs creative thinking; while the results of one analysis may suggest revisiting a prior analysis, a new conclusion may influence an old one.

Those arts organizations that design and pursue coherent planning processes support the development of rigorous analyses that result in the creation of creative, effective strategies.

THE PLANNING ENVIRONMENT

16

The way a planning process is implemented will depend, in great measure, on the situation facing the organization when it decides to develop the plan. Only a few arts organizations have the discipline to develop comprehensive strategic plans in a rigorous way during periods of stability. Most organizations embark on planning exercises when facing a period of change owing to financial distress, discontinuity in operations (including physical expansion), the loss of a major funder, new senior staff, or the decision to pursue a serious stabilization effort.

FINANCIAL DISTRESS

The most common reason that arts organizations turn to planning is the onset of significant financial problems. When there is considerable cash flow pressure, when nothing suggests that this pressure will abate, when every conversation revolves around cash shortages, when the fun of involvement has evaporated, and when the board and the staff have no solutions, arts organizations frequently turn to planning. (Of course, a well-implemented plan developed three years earlier may have averted the crisis.)

A plan meant to address a fiscal crisis must be comprehensive but must also be developed with dispatch. These plans accomplish several objectives:

- They force a discussion on the root problems facing the organization.
- They encourage a logical, organized discussion of possible solutions.
- They create alignment of the board and staff around a true mission and a course of action.
- They result in a document that can be used to attract new board members and donors.
- They can be used with funders to help show how additional investment in the institution will contribute to long-term stability.

What the plan will *not* do is solve the cash flow problem. This will be accomplished only if the plan is implemented. This typically takes a great deal of *disciplined* effort and by board and staff. If the effort devoted to creating the plan exhausts the time and energy commitment of the key participants, leaving no resources for implementation, it is certain to have no impact on the institution.

Too often, even when a troubled organization does work hard to create and implement a plan, the focus is placed solely on the short-term fiscal needs. The temptation to solve this most pressing problem is understandable, but the longer-term consequences can be significant. Troubled organizations often look for an angel: someone who will make a huge gift and "solve" the problem. Often the hoped-for angel has no relationship with the organization, making the chance of a life-changing gift very remote. In fact, there are very few institutions that are saved simply by an infusion of short-term cash. While mounting an emergency campaign is frequently a central part of the strategy for a troubled institution, it cannot be the only area of focus. Without addressing methods for increasing both earned and contributed income by building a larger family of supporters, and controlling costs, the organization is likely to experience serious cash flow problems yet again when the short-term campaign revenue is depleted. Many organizations have to learn how to reduce expenses. Even more have to learn how to enhance income generation by employing sophisticated marketing and fund-raising techniques. The payoff from these approaches is not achieved in the near term; the best arts leaders will make the effort to ensure that long-term revenue growth is pursued even in the face of daunting short-term crises.

PHYSICAL EXPANSION

When a major expansion is under consideration, the planning calendar can be a bit more relaxed. But the case for pursuing a broad planning effort is just as compelling. Too often, organizations in this situation look simply at the design of the facility, the cost of construction, and the feasibility of the campaign. Too little time is spent reviewing what is needed for a smooth transition to the new space, the marketing, fund-raising, and other operating requirements for supporting that facility and the impact of the expansion and the campaign on the staff and board.

In fact, many organizations begin serious strategic planning only after designs for the new building are completed. This leaves little room for the planning process to affect the design. While the excitement generated around architectural drawings is significant and understandable, arts organizations must discipline themselves to complete major planning processes *before* any designs are initiated. This allows the plan to address the marketing, staffing, board expansion, and fund-raising issues that must be solved before a major expansion. It also allows the campaign to be specified more accurately by including all the costs the expansion will incur, not simply the capital costs. Yet too many boards and staffs get so excited about the facility design (an *edifice complex*) that serious, rigorous, organized planning efforts fall by the wayside.

LOSS OF MAJOR FUNDERS

Like organizations in fiscal crisis, those that lose the support of a major funder have waited too long to plan. Unless there is flexibility to reduce expenses in the short term (assuming the fund-raising and earned-income efforts cannot be expanded in the very short term), the financial implications will be substantial.

The answer to the loss of a major funder is not to seek a single replacement funder. Rather, the organization must find a way to enhance its visibility or to exploit its current visibility to attract a larger family of funders.

Working actively to strengthen the board is frequently an important element of this strategy. As mentioned previously, the plan itself will provide one of the most potent tools for soliciting new board members. The plan gives board prospects a clear picture of the direction of the organization and the way their efforts will be helpful. Those prospects from the corporate sector will be familiar with business plans and will appreciate the rigor of the planning process.

CHANGES IN LEADERSHIP

When an organization experiences changes at the highest level of the board or the staff, the plan becomes an important transition tool. The new leaders can use the planning process to create a renewed sense of direction and vitality, effectively addressing the organizational insecurities that attend any change in leadership. This is particularly true when a visionary leader leaves the institution; new leaders must be given the opportunity to create their own platform. A substantial institutional marketing campaign focused on the new leader is one way to ensure a smoother transition.

STABILIZATION

Some planning processes are undertaken when an arts organization decides to make an effort to achieve long-term financial stability. (Frequently a special gift from a major donor inspires this decision.) Stabilization is one of the best reasons for embarking on a planning process.

Yet stabilization requires more than financial analysis and a campaign plan. The definition of a stabilization strategy must be broadened to include the operational actions that create financial security in the arts. Simply erasing an accumulated deficit, building an endowment, or creating a working capital reserve is not enough to stabilize an organization. The artistic, marketing, and development plans must also support the development of the family, leading to ongoing revenue growth.

Without long-term revenue growth, a stabilization campaign really provides only a few years of cash flow relief, not a bad thing but not real stabilization either.

NEW ORGANIZATIONS

Very few new arts organizations initiate any form of rigorous planning. The effort it takes to mount a first production or exhibition and the limited availability of money and managerial expertise make it difficult to think about the future in an organized manner.

Unfortunately, the failure to think of the first production or exhibition as part of a continuum can be quite costly. Donors and ticket purchasers who support the first performances are not adequately engaged, people who can provide support in the future are not asked to attend, and members of the press are not cultivated for future coverage.

While developing a comprehensive long-term plan for a new arts organization may not be justified, or even possible, a simple two-year plan can be very effective. Evaluating environmental opportunities and constraints and developing basic strategies for dealing with them can help set priorities, attract board members, and convince institutional donors that this new company is approaching its future in an intelligent manner.

Regardless of the situation facing an arts organization, plans are only as effective as the people who create and implement them. Employing sophisticated planning techniques is considerably less important than finding the best people to develop strategies and manage their implementation. Yet, armed with strong analytical techniques and a logical planning framework, a well-managed arts organization with an effective board and, most important, a dynamic and exciting artistic product can create plans that accomplish a wide range of initiatives.

In the end, however, it all comes down to probabilities. No one can promise that the building will be expanded, the tour will be enlarged, or the deficit will be erased — or that they won't. Turning your dreams into strategies simply increases the odds that they will come true.

ACKNOWLEDGMENTS

My approach to planning has been developed over the past forty years with tremendous assistance and input from too many people to name. I would especially like to thank W. Walker Lewis who taught me the fundamentals of planning when I knew literally nothing and Brett E. Egan, my colleague for the past eight years, who has changed my thinking on so many aspects of planning. Indeed, you can teach an old horse new tricks.

I would also like to recognize Victoria A. Bergeron, for her assistance in completing this book, and Phyllis Deutsch, of the University Press of New England, who played a leading role in publishing my last five books.

ALSO FROM MICHAEL M. KAISER

The Art of the Turnaround

Creating and Maintaining Healthy Arts Organizations

MICHAEL M. KAISER

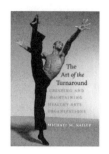

Practical advice (supported by extensive case studies)
for fixing troubled arts organizations

"This book is a valuable management resource; arts administrators could do worse than emulate Kaiser's work ethic, boldness of vision and ability to learn from mistakes. Those interested in keeping America's arts institutions vital ignore his insights at their peril."
—*Opera News*

"[An] extraordinary book that serves as both cautionary tale and practical primer in crisis response. . . . Whether you are serving in an entry level or executive leadership position, from crew chief to executive director, there is much to be learned from in Michael Kaiser's *The Art of the Turnaround*."
—*Theatre Design & Technology*

"Michael Kaiser, the 'Miracle Worker.' We know now we can expect miracles from Michael Kaiser, and in his wonderful new book he tells you how to do the same for your organization. Ten rules to his kind of success—that's what you'll find within the pages of *The Art of the Turnaround*."
—Barbara Cook

BRANDEIS UNIVERSITY PRESS
Published by University Press of New England
Hardcover ISBN: 978-1-58465-735-4
Ebook ISBN: 978-1-58465-814-6
www.upne.com

ALSO FROM MICHAEL M. KAISER

Leading Roles

50 Questions Every Arts Board Should Ask

MICHAEL M. KAISER

A concise, practical, and timely guide for board members
of arts organizations

"*Leading Roles* is a rich yet tidy cornucopia of solutions for the challenges facing
the American arts scene . . . The author is compelling as he scopes the horizon,
sizing up a future in which global cooperation will loom large for the arts."
—*Washington Post*

"Although aimed at associations in the arts—dance, opera, theatre—the book
Kaiser has written should be must-reading for every board member and staff
executive of every association. *Leading Roles* addresses every aspect of board
participation in the life of an association, including mission and governance;
fundraising and marketing; the relationship of the board to the artistic director,
executive director, and staff; and board responsibilities for planning and
budgeting."
—*The Examiner*, Washington, DC

"No one knows more about arts administration than Michael Kaiser. No wonder
people the world over clamor for his attention and keen advice. The Kennedy
Center's not-so-secret weapon is an international treasure. The book is a
goldmine."
—Terrence McNally, playwright

BRANDEIS UNIVERSITY PRESS
Published by University Press of New England
Hardcover ISBN: 978-1-58465-906-8
Ebook ISBN: 978-1-58465-951-8
www.upne.com

ALSO FROM MICHAEL M. KAISER

The Cycle

A Practical Approach to Managing Arts Organizations

MICHAEL M. KAISER WITH BRETT E. EGAN

Offers practical advice, based on the notion of a "family" of supporters, for managing healthy arts organizations

"The next best things to having Michael Kaiser, 'the turnaround king,' in one's office, may just be having a copy of *The Cycle: A Practical Approach to Managing Arts Organizations* on one's bookshelf. This third book in a trilogy affords palpable arts-managerial advice that takes on a different life with each read."
—*American Journal of Arts Management*

"The third in Kaiser's trilogy on managing arts organizations, this volume is prescriptive, straightforward, and realistic."
—*Publishers Weekly*

"Michael Kaiser has written an invaluable guide to managing arts organizations for success and sustainable growth. His clear insights are accompanied by a deliberate approach and simple tools specifically designed to help small and midsize arts organizations tackle what can otherwise feel like complicated and overwhelming tasks. Loaded with 'aha moments,' *The Cycle* should be read and reread as an ongoing resource that can be shared with colleagues."
—Anita Contini, Bloomberg Philanthropies

"Michael Kaiser has done it again: *The Cycle* is a road map for arts organizations that want to connect their mission to their financial success. The book takes you through a step-by-step process that allows your artistic strengths to be leveraged into financial resources."
—Dennis Scholl, Knight Foundation

BRANDEIS UNIVERSITY PRESS
Published by University Press of New England
Hardcover ISBN: 978-1-61168-400-1
Ebook ISBN: 978-1-61168-478-0
www.upne.com

ALSO FROM MICHAEL M. KAISER

Curtains?

The Future of the Arts in America

MICHAEL M. KAISER

A passionate and provocative assessment of the decline
of performing arts institutions in the United States and
how to save them

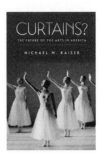

"While a critical statement to the field at a critical time, *Curtains?* has plenty for
anyone curious about what gets on stage, what doesn't, and why. If you ever
looked up in an orchestra hall and marveled at all of the missing bodies, you
will find this a satisfying read. In a single, compelling 145-page breath, Kaiser
clears up the mystery and remains one of the few who doesn't stint on the
gory details." —*Philadelphia Inquirer*

"Of particular interest to the leaders of struggling companies will be [Kaiser's]
detailed thoughts on building more supportive and effective boards containing
members with a broad range of expertise, background and even income levels.
Only with such diverse and active boards, he contends, can arts organizations
do the long-range planning necessary to survive in today's challenging
environment." —*Washington Post*

"Just as wealth and power are increasingly concentrated amongst a shrinking
number of powerful individuals and corporations, [Kaiser] sees a few famous
mega-institutions dominating what's left of the arts landscape, sucking
up the talent and attention, catering to the wealthy who can underwrite
their productions and afford their tickets. As the number of small and midsize groups shrinks, he predicts, so will the ethnic diversity and artistic
experimentation that brings us the next defining trend or great artist, since
the mega-troupes will have to appeal to the widest possible audience (at least
in their online, mass offerings.)" —*Miami Herald*

"In his new book, former Kennedy Center impresario Michael Kaiser argues that
the future of the arts lies with quality, subsidy, and daring—all of which are in
dangerously short supply." —*American Theatre*

BRANDEIS UNIVERSITY PRESS
Published by University Press of New England
Hardcover ISBN: 978-1-61168-703-3
Ebook ISBN: 978-1-61168-704-0
www.upne.com